THE CHRISTIAN DOCTRINE OF GRACE

THE CHRISTIAN DOCTRINE OF GRACE

By

OSCAR HARDMAN, M.A., D.D.

PROFESSOR OF PASTORAL AND LITURGICAL THEOLOGY IN THE
UNIVERSITY OF LONDON,
WARDEN OF KING'S COLLEGE THEOLOGICAL HALL, AND
EXAMINING CHAPLAIN TO THE BISHOP OF LONDON

LONDON
JOHN HERITAGE
THE UNICORN PRESS

Made in Great Britain. Printed by SHERRATT & HUGHES, at the St. Ann's
Press, Manchester

TO
LORNA NICOLE
CHILD OF GRACE

CONTENTS

CHAPTER I

THE HISTORY OF THE FORMULATION OF
THE DOCTRINE

Two considerations might well deter the hesitant reader from the study of a book on the doctrine of grace. First, the doctrine is profound in its nature, wide in its scope, comprehensive in its bearings, forbidding in its possession of a technical terminology, and confusing in the variety of the formulations which its successive exponents have given to it. It is the work of the most acute and penetrating minds among all those whose services the Church has been able to claim; and it demands the close and serious attention of any who would seek to understand it. And secondly, the fact that it is not embodied in the Church's creeds may suggest that it is not of primary importance. As Dr. Headlam has said, this doctrine " has never been expressed in the creeds as part of the Catholic faith. . . . It is interesting to notice, for example, that when Pelagianism was condemned and a statement of what was believed to be the Christian faith was made by various councils, no attempt was made to include that in any statement of the faith which was imposed upon people for acceptance. It became part of the theological tradition of the Church, and so influenced its prayers and teaching and life, but it did not become part of the doctrine necessary for Church membership."

Over against these arguments, however, there are one or two good reasons to be given for the encouragement of any who are considering the reading of such a book as this. Though the doctrine is not included in the creed, it serves to relate and to illumine many of the doctrines which are so included. It may even be said that to ignore the doctrine of grace is to restrict oneself inevitably to a superficial understanding of the creeds. Further, the doctrine provides a necessary corrective to that Pelagian, or self-sufficient, outlook on life which seems to be natural to all vigorous peoples; and it is to be noted that it has received but scant attention in the recent history of the Church of England. And finally, conflicting interpretations of this doctrine constitute one of the chief causes of division between Catholics and Protestants; and it is the duty of all who would contribute in any way to the work of re-uniting the divided Church to try to understand the grounds of the opposition.

A brief treatment of so vast and complex a subject as this, which is very fittingly included in a Christian Challenge series, can be of little use unless it is methodical. Lack of method is likely to prove more serious here than in any other department of theological inquiry. The historical method of exposition, by which the story of the classic debates on the subject is unfolded in chronological order, is the first to suggest itself to a writer: but this method has recently been employed by Dr. N. P. Williams in a small but invaluable book entitled *The Grace of God*, to which the readers of this book are strongly recommended to give their attention. It remains for one who would cover the same ground by a different method, in the hope of assisting readers to a further understanding of a large matter, to give separate treatment to the various problems which make up the whole doctrine, prefacing the chapters in which these separate studies are found by a rapid historical survey which will serve to ' place ' the theologians subsequently referred to, and to suggest the settings of their various doctrinal systems. This introductory chapter is to be regarded, therefore, as the barest outline of the history of the formulation of the doctrine of grace, to be developed in the fuller consideration of specific problems in the chapters which follow.

Our starting-point is the New Testament. The Greek word *charis*, which is translated ' grace ', occurs in these scriptures about one hundred and fifty times. This frequent use of the term is very largely due to St. Paul, who finds occasion to introduce it into his epistles in no fewer than one hundred places. Applying to God a word which was used by his contemporaries to denote the imperial favour by which gifts were bestowed upon the cities and peoples of the Empire—commonly with a strong suggestion of god-like beneficence, and occasionally with a hint at mystic or magical power—St. Paul writes exultingly of the grace which he has himself received from a yet higher source. Chosen for this entirely undeserved favour from before the beginning of time, as he believes, he has been delivered from a hopeless state of bondage to the law, and from the spiritual blindness in which he has persecuted the Church; and, having been freely justified, he has been privileged to become the devoted bond-servant of Christ and an heir of glory. The same grace which has thus transformed him from a slave to a free man will avail, he asserts, for the deliverance of all who, like himself, have been fore-ordained in the counsels of God to this state of salva-tion. God is " the King of kings and Lord of lords "; and that royal beneficence which men attribute to earthly rulers when they are seen to exercise their prerogative of bestowing favours upon their subjects is proclaimed by St. Paul to be truly characteristic of Him who is " the blessed and only Potentate ". In his Epistle to the Romans in particular he has given us the classic statement of his belief concerning the grace of God; and this letter has served as the foundation of the Church's development of the doctrine and, together with the writings of St. Augustine, as the chief armoury of those who have shared in the con-troversies which it has provoked.

This development and these controversies belong to the West. Eastern Christians lived the life of grace, and those who taught and defended the Faith in the early centuries made frequent reference to the grace by which they lived: but no serious controversies arose among them concerning its scope and the manner of its operation, and the doctrine consequently remained descriptive in form, never achieving the fullness and precision with which it was formulated in the West. Even in St. John Chrysostom, the leading Eastern exponent of the doctrines of grace and free will, this lack of system is plainly seen. God's grace was held to be available for all men, in aid of the free will which belonged to their nature. The Church of Christ, to which men were admitted by the ' seal ' of initiation, was believed to be the especial scene of the bestowal of grace. And in the Church the sanctity of life which characterised its members, and the courage which sometimes issued in martyrdom, were recognised as the gifts of grace, as were also the special abilities and graces of individual members of the Church, both ordained and lay. This primitive and simple ' orthodoxy ' in respect of the doctrine of grace has persisted in the Eastern Church down to the present day.

In the West, on the contrary, there was an early development of interest in the related problems of sin and grace. This was stimulated by the barbarian invasions of the Empire and the signs of its approaching dissolution; and the development of the Pauline doctrine of grace moved rapidly forward to the extended and masterly exposition of the subject which was made by St. Augustine in the early years of the fifth century.

This movement of thought was initiated by Tertullian, the zealous and brilliant North African, who died in about the year 230; and he largely determined the lines which it was to follow. Believing that the soul is material, and that both the body and the soul of a child are generated by its parents, he concluded that the propagation of the soul carries with it the transmission of that corruption of the soul which is effected by sin. Thus the sin of Adam and Eve was held by him to be responsible for the production of injurious consequences in all human souls, and to call for the operation of God's grace. Whereas St. Paul had opposed 'grace' to 'works', that is to say, the conception of the free gift of God to the idea of merit earned by man's obedience to the law, Tertullian set 'grace' over against 'nature', by which he meant human nature bearing upon it the marks of the Fall. And, while he did not regard that nature as wholly corrupt or as completely deprived of the power of moral choice, he emphasised the need and the supremacy of grace so as to minimise greatly, though not altogether to deny, man's capacity for self-determination. Further, he wrote of grace as a spiritual power in such a way as to suggest its existence in detachment from God and almost so as to constitute it an impersonal force.

Towards the middle of the third century St. Cyprian, Bishop of Carthage, taught that grace is the reward of loyalty, and that, while God's grace is sufficient for the salvation of all who are baptised, there is in it no irresistible control of man's will. Lactantius (d. 325) followed St. Cyprian in representing grace as the reward of merit; St. Hilary of Poitiers (d. 368) supported the opinion that man is himself able to initiate that act of turning to God which meets with the reward of grace; and St. Ambrose, Bishop of Milan, who died in 397, inclined to the same view, though he taught that the divine image had been lost to man by the Fall, and that all the descendants of Adam possessed a sinful nature and shared the guilt of Adam's sin. The Hilary who was known as Ambrosiaster moved away from that recognition of the persistence of some remnant of goodness and power in fallen man which had hitherto characterised the teaching of theologians in East and West alike; and he developed the idea of man's inability to make the initial step towards his recovery.

Then came Pelagius and the great St. Augustine. The former was a British monk living an ascetic life in Rome at the time when St. Augustine's *Confessions* appeared, shortly after the year 400. The latter was a man who had been converted to Christianity in 386, when he was thirty-two years of age, and consecrated in 395 to be Bishop of Hippo in North Africa, where he worked with great energy and devotion until his death in the year 430. Pelagius was moved by the apathy of many of his fellow-Christians to a crusade of encouragement and urgent exhortation. He sought to rouse men from their dangerous self-complacency, and to stimulate them to the task of working out their own salvation with fear and trembling by the exercise of that will-power which they possessed but were guiltily failing to use. St. Augustine also had taught

that man's will is free to enable him to turn to God:
but his study of St. Paul in the light of his own experience of conversion had caused him to lay increasing
stress upon the grace by which man's deliverance is
effected. A deep conviction of sin, and a strong sense
of God's extraordinary mercy in delivering him from
his evil way of life, combined with his observation of
the social and political ills of the time to produce in
him a growing tendency to regard man as incapable
of taking any share, however small, in the work of his
redemption, and to ascribe it wholly to the operation
of God's grace.

In his *Confessions* St. Augustine, out of his sense of
utter dependence upon God, had written the prayer
" Give what Thou commandest, and command what
Thou willest ". These words were quoted in the hearing of Pelagius; and thus the long controversy between
the two men was begun. Pelagianism, which was
developed by Pelagius with the help of his friend
Coelestius, and later by the young Bishop Julian of
Eclanum, started with the initial advantage of simplicity—a simplicity which was achieved by presenting
some of the facts of human life and ignoring the rest.
Augustinianism, which was gradually developed by
St. Augustine as he put his whole strength into the
safeguarding of his position under the stress of controversy, and as it was still further developed after his
death by Lucidus, was an attempt, foredoomed to
failure, to take account of all the facts and to combine
them in a system which yielded nothing to Pelagianism

in coherence and clearness. But the Church condemned Pelagianism, as it was bound to do; and, though it has never accepted systematised Augustinianism, it has consistently approved the general position of St. Augustine as against that of Pelagius.

Realising that, while St. Augustine insisted upon the freedom of man's will in a limited and particular sense, he taught in effect that the Fall had deprived him of so much of his original endowment that nothing but the grace of God could reclaim and sanctify him, and that this saving grace was a free gift bestowed or withheld by God's sovereign right, Pelagius feared that men would be delivered from all sense of the need for effort in the moral life. He maintained that there had been no Fall in consequence of Adam's sin, except in Adam himself, and that the human will remains altogether free; that righteousness can be achieved by man's endeavour; and that the grace of God, which is seen primarily in the bestowal of man's natural gifts, is to be regarded further as no more than the conveyance of forgiveness of sins by baptism, and the provision of supplementary and external aids to human effort in the form of instruction and example.

The controversy between the two men and their supporters was carried from Rome to Carthage, from Carthage to Palestine, and from Palestine back to Rome and Carthage, between the years 409 and 418. At the beginning it was mainly an attack on Augustine's doctrine conducted by Pelagius and Coelestius, St. Augustine himself refraining from a counter-attack

B

because he recognised the good intention and zeal of Pelagius, and because he was much occupied with other matters. In 412, however, he began to give himself seriously to the work of exposing what was clearly becoming a dangerous heresy, and he addressed to Marcellinus a treatise entitled *On the Merits and Forgiveness of Sins, and the Baptism of Infants*. This was followed rapidly by an answer to a question raised by Marcellinus, St. Augustine dispatching a work *On the Spirit and the Letter* before the end of the year. In 415 he produced *On Nature and Grace* in direct reply to a work of Pelagius entitled *On Nature*, and he added *On Man's Perfection in Righteousness* in answer to certain propositions said to have been put forth by Coelestius. In 417, after Pelagius had been acquitted of heresy by a Palestinian tribunal, St. Augustine addressed to Bishop Aurelius of Carthage a treatise entitled *On the Proceedings of Pelagius*.

Though Pelagius received much support, especially in the East, where there was a distinct unwillingness to define closely the respective spheres of grace and free will, the doctrine of St. Augustine was approved by the Council of Carthage in 418, and was admitted by Pope Zosimus who, as a Greek, with Eastern prejudices, had previously decided in favour of Pelagius.

The Church has endorsed the decision of the Council of Carthage with complete consistency throughout its subsequent history, finding no place for Pelagianism within its doctrinal system. A system of thought which so completely detaches the creature from the

Creator, giving him a virtual independence in forget-fulness of the fact that " In him we live, and move, and have our being ", is entirely alien to it. On the other hand, Augustinianism, which rightly insists upon the creatureliness of man, is left to wrestle with the insoluble problem of reconciling the omnipotence of God with the reality of man's self-consciousness and individual experience; and the subsequent history of the formulation of the doctrine of grace shows a succession of movements to the left and to the right —towards allowing man some real power of self-direction and towards making him the undeserving favourite or the helpless victim of arbitrary divine decree—St. Augustine being drawn upon by the dispu-tants in each movement, and interpreted either less strictly than some of his words require or more harshly than the sum total of his teaching justifies.

After the Council of Carthage St. Augustine was engaged by opponents on two sides. The gifted Julian, Bishop of Eclanum in southern Italy, took up the cudgels on behalf of Pelagianism and belaboured St. Augustine with shrewd blows and great force; while among the monks of Adrumetum in Africa, and of Lerins in southern Gaul, where Pelagius was un-compromisingly repudiated, Augustine was openly criticised and corrected.

In the year 418 St. Augustine examined the most recent teaching of Pelagius and Coelestius in a work entitled *On the Grace of Christ and on Original Sin*. A treatise *On Marriage and Concupiscence*, which was

written in 419, having been subjected to severe criticism
by Julian, St. Augustine added to it a second book on
the same subject in 420. In the same year he produced
On the Soul and its Origin, in correction of the errors
of a young African named Vincentius Victor, and a
treatise *Against Two Letters of the Pelagians*, one of
which was written by Julian and the other by a number of bishops among whom Julian was included. In
421 he wrote *Against Julian*; and to Julian's reply to
this he planned an exhaustive answer, which he
left unfinished at his death. A year later, in 431,
Pelagianism was again condemned, by the Council of
Ephesus.

On the other side of attack John Cassian of Massilia
(*d.* 435), author of the *Institutes* and the *Conferences*,
was the chief spokesman of a group of theologians in
southern Gaul who opposed the doctrine of the
irresistibility of grace and insisted on finding a place
in human nature for a small measure of self-determination, in spite of the admittedly disastrous results of the
Fall. The freedom which they claimed for man was
much more limited than that which was claimed by
Pelagius; and in all cases of sudden conversion it was
allowed by Cassian, who had no knowledge of the
gradualness of the processes which lead to such seem-
ing suddenness in the final crisis, that everything must
be conceded to the operation of grace. Thus he taught
what has been known since the sixteenth century as
Semi-Pelagianism, the characteristic note of which is
the claim that man has the power to turn to God and

so to invite and, as it were, to initiate the operation of grace.

To the monks of Adrumetum St. Augustine addressed a treatise *On Grace and Free Will* in the year 426, and a further work, *On Rebuke and Grace*, in the following year. To his friends Prosper and Hilary, two laymen of Aquitania, who had reported to him the similar opposition to his teaching which existed among the monks of southern Gaul, he sent in 428 a work entitled *On the Predestination of the Saints*, and in 429 a second treatise, *On the Gift of Perseverance*.

After his death a year later, Prosper continued St. Augustine's work of exposition and defence, first answering in detail the sixteen objections to St. Augustine's teaching which were put forth by Vincentius, and then replying to Cassian in a work called *Against the Author of the Conferences*. Prosper was succeeded by Lucidus, a presbyter of Gaul, who held extreme predestinarian views: but these he was persuaded to repudiate when, in 475, he appeared before the Council of Arles at the citation of Faustus, Bishop of Riez. This Faustus, who had been formerly the head of the monastery of Lerins, subsequently wrote, at the request of the Council, a work entitled *On Grace and Free Will*, in which he expounded Semi-Pelagian views.

The issue between Augustinianism and Semi-Pelagianism was determined not long after by the efforts of Caesarius, Bishop of Arles from 501: but, though Augustine prevailed over Cassian, the influence of the Massilian school of theologians was seen when the controversy was closed, for the time, by Rome's adoption of the findings of the small Second Council of Arausio (Orange), which met in the year 529. This Council approved once more the Augustinian position as against the Pelagian: but, while it rejected the chief tenet of Semi-Pelagianism, its statement of Augustinianism was couched in a distinctly modified form. It repudiated the doctrine of predestination to eternal death, to which St. Augustine had committed himself in effect, though not by explicit statement, in his teaching concerning ' preterition '; it refrained from pronouncing upon the doctrine of the irresistibility of grace; and it recognised the existence of a certain ability in man to co-operate with divine grace after the work of grace had been initiated within him.

An attempt on the part of a Gallican monk, Gottschalk of Orbais (*d.* 869), to revive Augustinianism in its severest form led to a controversy on the subject of predestination in the middle of the ninth century. Gottschalk, who taught the doctrine of ' double predestination '—the predestination of some to life and, just as deliberately, of the others to death—was opposed by Rabanus Maurus, Archbishop of Mainz, and was condemned by the Council of Mainz in 848. His case was then further debated between Remigius, Archbishop of Lyons, and Hincmar, Archbishop of Rheims; and Gottschalk's teaching was again condemned, at the instance of Hincmar, by two successive synods held at Quiercy, in 849 and 853 respectively. John Scotus Eriugena contributed to the controversy by writing a work *On Predestination*, at Hincmar's request; ·and this served to prolong the dissension, which did not cease until peace was made at the Synod of Tousy in 860.

At the end of the eleventh century St. Anselm (*d.* 1109) produced his great work on the doctrine of the Atonement, *Why was God made Man?* in which he embodied a modified Augustinianism, emphasising the truth that all grace is to be attributed to the redeeming work of Christ, whose merits are available for transference to men. A little later St. Bernard wrote his treatise *Concerning Grace and Free Will* (*c.* 1128), in which he renewed the attribution of grace to the work of the incarnate Christ, and taught that man's part in the work of redemption consists solely in his consent to the operation of grace. And in the same century Peter Lombard (*d.* 1160), while accepting the Augustinian position, made a new departure by explicitly identifying grace with the Person of the Holy Spirit.

In the thirteenth century Augustinianism was challenged anew by the Franciscan schoolmen. The attempts made by Alexander of Hales (*d.* 1245) and St. Bonaventura (*d.* 1274) to save something from the wreck of human nature which had been produced by the Fall were continued with greater daring by their successor Duns Scotus (*d.* 1308), who advanced the contention that the sin of Adam had resulted only in the loss of certain original and special endowments of human nature such as immortality and freedom from pain, and that by the exercise of the free will which remained to him man could merit the bestowal of the grace of God. The difficulty of the introduction of the idea of merit was met by the invention of a distinction between merit which is 'condign', or wholly deserving, and merit which is only 'congruous', or appropriate.

The Franciscans were opposed by St. Thomas Aquinas (d. 1274), who formulated the famous distinction between 'actual grace' and 'habitual grace', and by other learned Dominicans; and the work of these supporters of a stricter Augustinianism was continued by such men as Thomas of Bradwardine (d. 1349) and John Wyclif (d. 1384) among the secular clergy. But in spite of the strength of their advocacy Augustinianism steadily lost ground as the Middle Ages wore on to a close, the doctrine of merit playing an increasingly large part in the practical working of the Church's system.

The violent return to Augustinianism in its strictest form, and the great stress laid upon the doctrine of justification by faith, which characterised the protest of the Reformers in the sixteenth century, led to the reconsideration of the whole subject at the earlier sessions of the Council of Trent (1545–63); and as a result the differences of the Augustinian and the Semi-Pelagian elements on the Catholic side were composed in a verbal compromise which suggested the retention of the full Augustinian position but at the same time allowed for those modifications in the position which had been accepted by the Church since the days of the Council of Orange. In particular there was a marked revision of St. Augustine's teaching concerning the nature of Adam and the consequences of his sin; and it was declared that the Fall did not completely rob man of his free will, but that it only weakened it and predisposed it to the choice of evil.

That was the end of unmitigated Augustinianism in the Church of Rome, in spite of the nominal adherence which continues to be given to it under the name Augustinism; and since the publication of the Tridentine decisions it has been condemned whenever it has raised its head. Thus in 1567 Franciscan influence secured the condemnation of Baius, who included some elements of rigid Augustinianism in his strangely confused system of doctrine; and in the seventeenth century the system of thought which took its name from Cornelius Jansen, Bishop of Ypres, (*d.* 1638), and was subsequently associated with the names of Pascal and Quesnel, was rejected as a revival of the heresy of Baius. On the other hand, the Dominicans failed to secure the condemnation of a work written by the Spanish Jesuit, Luis de Molina, in 1588, entitled *The Concord of Free Will with Divine Prescience, Providence, Predestination, and Reprobation*, although it departed unmistakably from true Augustinianism in its insistence upon the freedom of the will; and Molinism is still current in the Roman Church of to-day, together with a modified form of it, known as

Congruism, which resulted from the efforts of Suarez and others to bring it nearer to the Augustinian position.

The Protestant Reformers found in the Augustinian doctrine of grace, robbed of every balancing consideration and pressed remorselessly to its extremest conclusions, the sharpest weapon with which to oppose the Church that claimed to uphold that doctrine but, by its practical system of meritorious works, seemed to them to be the exponent of pure Pelagianism. In his use of this weapon Martin Luther (*d.* 1546) gave prominence to the doctrine of determinism, contending that man's will was altogether incapacitated by the Fall and that nothing but the grace of God can move and equip him for the exercise of that faith by which he surrenders himself wholly and is accordingly justified. John Calvin (*d.* 1564) stressed particularly the doctrine of double predestination, boldly asserting the logical conclusion of St. Augustine's doctrine of preterition, and proclaiming that all men are either elect or condemned, according to the good pleasure and the righteous determination of their Creator.

But the divisions which date back to the fifth century soon declared themselves. Serious opposition was raised in both camps, by Melanchthon (*d.* 1560) among the Lutherans, and by Arminius (*d.* 1609) among the Reformed. Melanchthon, who had moved gradually away from the true Lutheran position, taught that man must be accounted to have in himself some power of turning to God and co-operating with Him, a belief which was then first termed 'synergism' (co-operation) as against 'monergism' (the sole work of God). Arminius declared that, though the initial work of reclaiming man must be attributed to God alone, man is himself capable of making a subsequent contribution towards the working out of his salvation. This was set forth in the famous *Remonstrance* of 1610 by his followers, who were condemned by the Calvinist Synod of Dort (Dordrecht) held in 1618–19.

The Barthian Theology of Crisis on the Continent to-day, which is seeking to promote a return to the doctrines of the sovereignty and the grace of God as these were formulated by the Protestant Reformers, reminds us that those doctrines have been very seriously weakened among Protestants by the Rationalism of the eighteenth century and the Scientific Humanism of the nineteenth century. The sternest form of Calvinism has persisted in places and has continued to propagate itself throughout the process of that intellectual disintegration of the Christian Faith which followed upon the work of the Continental Reformation: but, on the whole, its influence has steadily declined, and those Christian bodies which find themselves bound more or less rigidly by sixteenth- and seventeenth-century formularies giving expression to fundamental Calvinism are increasingly subject to disturbance by the troubled consciences of individual members of their societies. English Nonconformity and Scottish Presbyterianism have reason to know of this difficulty in connection with the *Westminster Confession* of 1643, which gives special attention to the subjects that bear upon the doctrine of grace.

In the Church of England a remarkable balance was achieved, in that the Book of Common Prayer breathed in general a chastened Augustinianism, while the Thirty-nine Articles avoided the unscriptural certainties of Calvinism so successfully as to win the support of the English Arminians in their debates with the unsatisfied Puritans in the seventeenth century. The Anglican pulpit has used its greater measure of freedom to proclaim the various shades of doctrine ranging from extreme Calvinism in the days of Elizabeth, through the Arminianism of the seventeeth-century divines and of Wesley and his Methodists in the eighteenth century, to the unashamed Pelagianism of the nineteenth and twentieth centuries, the modified Augustinianism of the Book of Common Prayer finding expression all the while, no doubt, in certain places. To-day it is not infrequently remarked by observers from without who do us the honour of visiting and reporting on our Church that we have an Augustinian Prayer Book and a Pelagian pulpit, and that few seem to be aware of the inconsistency. If this is true, it provides a very strong recommendation to the renewed study of the doctrine of grace.

CHAPTER II

THE GRACE OF THE LORD JESUS CHRIST

IT was stated above that the doctrine of grace, though not included in the creeds, serves to illumine the doctrines which are found there, because of the close relation which it bears to many of them. It has the nature of a co-ordinating doctrine, linking together all the foundation truths of the Christian religion. Its scope is thus seen to be very wide; and any attempt to gain a general understanding of the work and the nature of grace must reckon with the necessity of surveying a vast field, such a field, in fact, as is suggested by St. Paul's familiar phrase, " The grace of the Lord Jesus Christ ". This phrase attaches the idea of grace to the central doctrine of our Faith, round which the whole content of our belief is grouped; and it thereby indicates that, if we would know what grace is, we must consider the Nature of God and the nature of man, the character of the situation in which the Incarnation of the Son of God and His atoning Death upon the Cross became necessary, the significance of His Death and Resurrection and the result which was achieved by them, and the divine provision by which that act of God continues to be applied and extended.

A convenient approach to this vast subject may be

made by the examination and comparison of three phrases which have to do with the Nature of God and His relations with the universe. These are the Love of God, the Providence of God, and the Grace of God.

All three phrases must be understood to denote, in the first place, aspects or attributes or qualities belonging to the Nature of God, apart from any consideration of their exercise in His dealings with Creation; though it must at once be added that our knowledge of them is inevitably limited to what may be learned through that exercise. We cannot know God as He is in Himself, but only as He reveals Himself in His relations with us His creatures and with the world in which He has placed us. What we know of His Love and Providence and Grace is what we have received through revelation, which is a part of their use, or through experience of their action in ourselves and reflection upon it, or through observation of a corresponding activity in the lives of others and reflection upon their report of it. But from our knowledge of its active expression toward Creation we believe that God is Love, in the sense that is demanded and fulfilled by the revealed constitution of His Triune Being. We believe that there is in Him not only omniscience but also perfect Providence, or foreseeing, in the sense that He possesses an ability to view all things from the standpoint of eternity, and therefore to gather them up in an eternal ' now '. And we believe that He is full of Grace, in the original sense of the term which conveys the idea of surpassing loveliness and beauty of character.

When we consider the phrases in their bearing upon God's relations with the universe which He has created, we find that the Love of God must be held to carry the widest significance of the three. God's love is over all His works; and there is no part of the divine activity in calling the universe into being and in sustaining its dependent existence which does not properly fall within the exercise of His Love. There are, admittedly, certain phases of the operation of God's love which we are at a loss to account for in any completely satisfactory manner. There is the freedom that is enjoyed by destructive agencies; there are the apparent redundancies and extravagances which appear in the course of the development of life; there is the heavy burden of pain and suffering which is borne by animals and men. Only very partial explanations of these things are available in our present state of knowledge. But it is our faith, none the less, that God's love will vindicate itself at the last, and that we shall be fully assured by love's ultimate triumph that it has been operative throughout the confused process which now presents us with so many perplexing problems.

The Providence of God is a phrase which is generally used to mean that part of the operation of God's love which is concerned with the ordering of the external conditions of life in such a way as to advance the designs which it has formulated in its perfect wisdom from before the beginning of time. It is thought of as effective in the adaptation of all life to its environment, or conversely in the adaptation of environment to the needs of life; it contrives the structure and equipment of the countless organisms in which life is embodied; it prepares particular historical situations and introduces the right actors into those situations at the proper time; and it works by laws which are to a large extent concealed from man's observation, so that it is frequently necessary for him to acknowledge the limitations of his understanding by describing the operations of Providence as miraculous.

The Grace of God is not differentiated from the Providence of God in any agreed way. The two are intertwined to some extent, and they have been variously defined in their relation to each other. Initially they both refer to the hidden counsels of God, and they may be said to be almost identical in meaning when we use them in connection with the divine pre-determination of the operations of love. Subsequently, however, in their actual working, they are to be distinguished. The Grace of God is more limited in scope than the Providence of God, in that the former is restricted to mankind as the sphere of its operation, while the latter applies to the whole range of animate and inanimate Nature, though the governance of the fortunes and destinies of men is the aim which it has in view. In the particular sphere to which The Grace of God is restricted, however, it is wider than the Providence of God which operates there also, if, with

St. Augustine, we use it to cover both the internal and external operations of God's love. It is perhaps more common to use the Providence of God exclusively for the ordering of the external conditions of man's life, and to confine the Grace of God to the internal and secret operation wrought by the Spirit of God upon the spirit of man: but St. Augustine's use recognises more truly the interplay between external and internal and the impossibility of determining where Grace, if it is to be restricted to the internal, takes up the work of Providence.

The work of the Holy Spirit has been continuous throughout the history of man; for God is ever gracious, and His grace has ever rested upon man by the necessity which is included in the divine Nature. Before the Incarnation, however, God's favour was opposed by the sinfulness of man to so serious an extent that, when at length God made a way to overcome the opposition in the Person of His incarnate Son, it was as though the Holy Spirit had come to men for the first time, and as though the work of grace was but then begun. That is the reason why St. Paul speaks of "The grace of the Lord Jesus Christ". In the love and the providence of God it is by the instrumentality of the incarnate Son that the divine favour is delivered from the unbroken opposition with which it had formerly been met, and is now freely communicated to men. St. Paul's phrase sums up for us the full story of the divine purpose and achievement of the redemption of the human race.

C

Into the mystery of man's evil state we must make some brief inquiry at a later stage, when we come to consider the disability of the human nature upon which grace has to work: but the doctrine of grace is concerned not with the manner in which the problem of evil arose, but with its solution. God's love is challenged with frustration by the rebellion of the men and women whom He has created in His own image; and His grace, or ' radiant adequacy ' as it has been strikingly called, moves forth by the agency of the Holy Spirit for man's deliverance from ignorance and sin. " God so loved the world that He gave His only-begotten Son." Undertaking a new activity, while He yet maintains the universe as before, He effects the Incarnation of the Son, an act which is rendered possible by the affinity existing between God and man, according to the terms of man's creation. Jesus Christ is " conceived by the Holy Ghost, born of the Virgin Mary ". He does not convert the Godhead into flesh, but He takes the manhood into God. He makes no confusion or mingling of substances, or essential natures; there is no introduction of a new type intermediate between God and man, which is neither God nor man but a blend of both; and yet God and man become one Christ. This Jesus suffers for us men and for our salvation, offering in the name of the whole human family, of which He has become the true Head by virtue of His Incarnation, that perfect obedience to the laws of God for which man was created but which he has failed to yield. And out of the crisis of man's blasphemous opposition to God, involving Christ in a spiritual agony which passes our comprehension and yet successfully conveys the supreme appeal of God's love, He wins the means of reconciling the human family to God, claiming it one by one in the power of the new life which He communicates to it. Bursting the bonds of death and triumphing over the sin which constitutes its sting, He delivers the material Body from the corruption which death lays upon it, and translates it into the spiritual realm as the firstfruits of that redemption of the material order which is to be ultimately accomplished. To the little society of His followers, which is the Church, His Body, He sends, according to promise, the Holy Ghost, the Comforter, by whom the Grace of God is now to be bestowed in the fullness of measure which He has made possible, for communication to all who will accept in faith the Gospel of the Lord Jesus Christ and surrender themselves to be joined to Him mystically, sacramentally, and, by the continuing operation of grace, morally.

This is the work of grace. What is its nature? Remembering that it is " The grace of the Lord Jesus Christ ", or, as St. Augustine puts it, that " by which we are Christians ", and recalling the various interpretations of the nature of grace which have been advanced at various times, we have to inquire whether grace is the Holy Spirit who comes to make His abode with us; or the personal influence of Christ and the Spirit acting upon the persons of men by the way of suggestion and appeal; or some medicinal power which is imparted by God for the purifying and healing of the soul, some transforming gift conveyed to human nature by which every disorder is remedied, or something that has been lost is restored, or a new and additional equipment is added.

The identification of grace with the Person of the Holy Ghost is distinctly foreign to our accustomed way of thinking about it. But it was made in the eleventh of the Forty-two Articles of 1553, an Article which was omitted when the revision of 1563 took place and the Articles were reduced to thirty-nine in number. This Article was entitled *Of Grace*, and read as follows: " The grace of Christ, or the holie Ghost by him geuen, dothe take awaie the stonie harte, and geueth an harte of fleshe. And although those that haue no will to good thinges, he maketh them to wil, and those that would euil thinges, he maketh them not to wille the same: Yet neuerthelesse he enforceth not the wil. And therefore no man when he sinneth can excuse himself as not worthie to be blamed or condemned, by alleging that he sinned unwillinglie, or by compulsion." The desirability of making this identification once again has been urged recently by Dr. N. P. Williams in the book already referred to,[1] and it deserves careful consideration.

Looking back to the earliest days of the Church, when spirit-possession was a common mode of thought, we must regard it as inevitable that Christians, finding themselves possessed of newness of life and a variety

[1] *The Grace of God*, p. 110.

of striking gifts, should attribute the change that had taken place in them to the fact that they were indwelt by the Spirit of Christ in consequence of the divine grace or favour. The body of a Christian man was, as St. Paul expressed it, " a temple of the Holy Ghost ". As the personality of the Holy Spirit came to be more clearly apprehended, however, the power of the Christian life began to be attributed, by Tertullian first, to the grace which had been imparted by the Holy Spirit, rather than to ' possession ' by the Holy Spirit Himself.

Yet the Pauline figure of speech can never be abandoned; for it denotes most truly the intimacy of the relationship which is established between the Holy Spirit and the Christian soul. It is not surprising, therefore, that there is frequently found in the writings of Christian theologians a tendency to forget the distinction between ' grace ' and ' Spirit ', and actually to identify the two. Peter Lombard, who died in 1160, is instanced by Dr. Williams as having frankly made this identification; and he expresses the opinion that it would be advantageous if we could all agree to follow this lead. " I would suggest," he writes, " that our comprehension of grace will be enormously deepened and enriched if we take a step, on the verge of which, as we have seen, Christian theology has perpetually hovered, but which has actually been taken only by a few divines—namely, the frank equation of ' grace ' with the Person of the Holy Spirit. There are not two healing powers going forth from God, one personal and the other impersonal; nor is grace a quasi-material, something deposited in the soul by the Holy Spirit; there is only one glorious sanctifying Divine Power, which our Lord and His Apostles call the Spirit, but which we may, if we choose, name under the title of 'grace' (very much as the Jewish apocalyptists, from motives of reverence and to avoid a too frequent employment of the name of God, described the supreme Object of worship as 'the Great Glory'). If it be frankly recognised that 'the Spirit' and 'grace' are synonyms, we shall be able to recover the Pauline point of view concerning *pneuma* without jettisoning the familiar terminology of 'grace' now consecrated by the usage of well nigh seventeen centuries."

To this suggested identification Dr. J. K. Mozley demurs; and it may be considered probable that a majority of theologians will agree with him in his hesitation. "Close as is the connection between grace and the Holy Spirit," he says,[1] "I do not think that the New Testament allows of an absolute identification, while even though theology may have hovered on the brink of identification, it has always, as it seems to me, felt it necessary to leave room for a distinction."

There are further considerations to be adduced against the acceptance of the suggestion. If the grace of God, by which we are saved, is really to be identified with the Third Person of the Blessed Trinity, then it would appear that we have embarked upon the dangerous course of distributing the divine attributes between the three Persons and thus of overthrowing the doctrine of

[1] *The Gospel Sacraments*, p. 54.

the Trinity. As this doctrine stands, we must believe that the grace of God is the grace of Father, Son, and Holy Ghost. It is called " the grace of the Lord Jesus Christ " because, as we have considered, the Incarnation of the Son of God is its crowning expression; and it is specially associated with the Holy Ghost in the Christian experience because we live under the new dispensation consequent upon the accomplishment of Christ's redemptive work and His appointment of ' another Comforter '. But grace is, nevertheless, the grace of the indivisible Trinity and is not to be equated with any one Person of the Trinity. If it be objected that the grace of God may be regarded as practically equivalent to the love of God, and that, since God is Love, God is also Grace, and that therefore each Person of the Trinity may rightly be spoken of as Love or Grace, it must be acknowledged that this is true: but it must be added that it equally precludes the particular identification of grace with one Person of the Trinity, since ' grace ' must then be held to equal ' the Father ' or ' the Son ' as well as ' the Holy Ghost '.

Again, if the identification of ' grace ' and ' the Holy Ghost ' is advocated as a matter of convenience in terminology and of usefulness in checking the growth of impersonal and even materialistic conceptions of grace, it must be pointed out that it is more likely that there would be a distinct increase of danger in the opposite direction. The identification would almost certainly tend to increase the precariousness of the hold which many Christians have upon the doctrine of the personality of the Holy Spirit. The use of the terms ' Ghost ' and ' Spirit ' for the third Person of the Trinity and the lack of any helpful human analogy parallel to those of ' Father ' and ' Son ' in the case of the other two Persons, have always produced in the minds of untheological Christians a tendency to think of the Paraclete as an impersonal power; and this tendency could not fail to be increased if the Holy Spirit were now to be identified with grace. Instead of grace becoming personalised, Spirit would become depersonalised. Even for theologians themselves the abundance of reference to grace by writers who had not the slightest intention of obscuring the distinction between grace and the Holy Spirit would constitute a persistent suggestion that the doctrine of the personality of the Holy Ghost had been a mistake.

The fundamental objection to the proposal, however, is that the suggested equation would ignore the necessary distinction between a person and his personal influence. The influence that is exercised by one person upon another is the total effect of the suggestion and appeal, deliberate and unwilled, that goes forth from him in his association with the other. He may be truly said to ' spend himself ' and to ' give himself ' in the process of assistance and persuasion which he undertakes at times for the benefit of his friends: but the reference is clearly to the sacrificial quality of the activity performed and the exhausting nature of the service rendered, and not to any donation or transference of the person. Not only is the personality of the man who is using his influence not diminished thereby; it is enlarged and strengthened by such exercise. We are constrained to think in exactly the same way of the activity of the Holy Ghost, though the original perfection of Personality in God forbids us to entertain any suggestion of increase by activity. God the Holy Ghost consorts with the soul of a man and brings to bear upon him all the power that belongs to the Personality of God; and it is the influence which He exerts upon the man's soul that is the grace, not the Person who exerts the influence.

Finally, is grace to be wholly explained as 'influence'? Is it the case that, when we have fully reckoned with God's knowledge of the suggestibility of the human beings who are His handiwork, and with the wide range of means by which it is possible for Him to proffer to men suggestion calculated to stimulate them to right action, we have come to a complete understanding of the nature of grace? Or is there, perhaps, something that is medicinal in its quality and curative in its action; has it the nature of an elixir; may it be compared to a transfusion of blood for the re-invigoration of the life of a physical organism that is being destroyed by some hostile invasion?

It is probably true to say that a large number of Christian people still think of the soul as something included within the physical organism which is man's body. They give it no shape, it is true, nor do they locate it in the head or in the heart or in any other specified place; and it is certainly regarded by them as less substantial than any of the bodily organs. But none the less it is thought of as having a tenuous physical nature; it is a very vaguely conceived spiritual organism. The persistence of this belief is not surprising. It is the resultant of long ages of similar thought about ' spirits ', and it continues by reason of the extreme difficulty which is experienced by the human mind when it attempts to think of spiritual experience. Whenever we make a serious effort to explore the recesses of mind and personality, we find ourselves in danger of dissecting the powers and activities which we are considering, of giving them relative positions — as in the psychologists' division of the consciousness into subliminal and supraliminal, and even of labelling them as separate entities which tend to be regarded as ' portions ' making up the whole. In the mind of the untrained thinker there is no corrective to this kind of thing. Metaphor is used by him with no sense of its metaphorical character; and the language of ancient prayer, which was once innocent of metaphor to a majority of those who used it but has since become metaphorical, is still used by him as a statement of literal fact. Thus, when he prays that by the divine medicine " all the diseases of our souls may be healed ", he still thinks of the soul as substantial, of sin as the cause of a debilitating and corrupting disease of that part of him which is the soul, and of grace as a healing medicine bestowed by God through the agency of the Holy Spirit either directly or by the mediation of the Church. Having learned that, since the Incarnation effected a permanent union between God and man in the Person of Jesus Christ, man may be assimilated to the likeness of his Saviour by sacramental incorporation into the Body of Christ, he is able to think of grace as a quickening and transforming elixir, and to use with unsophisticated directness of speech and thought the words of the familiar and beautiful Collect which is found in the Gelasian Sacramentary: " O God, who at the beginning didst marvellously establish the dignity of man's substance, and hast now yet more marvellously restored the same: grant that we may be made partakers of his divine nature, who vouchsafed to become partaker of our human nature, who with thee and the Holy Ghost liveth and reigneth ever one God, world without end."

Soul and material substance, grace and transforming commodity, must, however, be regarded as incompatibles. We shall doubtless continue to speak of grace as being conveyed and infused, as healing the soul, and as transforming our nature: but we must repeatedly assure ourselves that these are figurative expressions by which we seek to convey what remains a profound mystery—the personal operation of the Spirit of God upon the spirit of man. What the spirit of man is we hardly know; much less do we know what the Spirit of God is. But we have no doubt that they are neither physical nor quasi-physical, and that their related action and reaction belong to the sphere of personal influence, exercised both with and without the use of physical agencies, as in all personal relation-ships.

The inner recesses of man's personality, which are reached by the Holy Spirit, have hitherto eluded the observation of the keenest observers. Mr. A. F. Shand has penetrated as far perhaps as any man, and his conclusion is recorded thus.[1] " Our personality does not seem to be the sum of the dispositions of our emotions and sentiments. These are our many selves; but there is also our one self. This enigmatical self which reflects on their systems, estimates them, and, however loath to do it, sometimes chooses between their ends, seems to be the central fact of our personality. If this be the fact, it is not the kind of fact which we can take into account. The science of character will be the science of our sentiments and emotions—of these many selves, not of this one self. It will try to under-stand those forces with which our personality has to reckon; but it will leave out of account the mystery which lies behind them."

Lest it should be supposed that ' influence ' is hardly adequate as a term to describe the fullness of the power of the Spirit in His dealings with the soul of man, it should be said that the term serves to guard the respon-sibility of man on the one hand, and that, on the other hand, it is not meant to limit, nor does it limit, God's power beyond the limitations which God has imposed upon Himself by the creation of man. ' In-fluence ' is a term which, when it is applied to God,

[1] *The Foundations of Character*, p. 66 f.

is necessarily extended to a degree which bears relation to the difference between the personality of man and the Personality of God. In proportion to the greatness of the personality, so is the influence that is exercised by it.

It is clear that the relationship between God and the human soul is very imperfectly illustrated by the analogy of the relationship between one human being and another. Human beings are separate from one another as God and man are not separate. Even in the case of two persons who are very closely related as members of the same family, and very understanding and sympathetic towards each other by virtue of strong emotional, intellectual, and spiritual affinities, they remain separate and independent centres of life throughout the course of their existence. A very strong measure of personal influence may be exercised by each upon the other: but neither of them can go beyond the limits of their respective personalities. When God deals with a soul, however, not only is perfect Personality introduced with all its richness of power, but He is dealing with a life which was created and is sustained by Him. That life has no existence apart from Him; and, though God allows to it such a degree of self-direction as to enable it to believe in its independence, it is obvious that it continues to exist, none the less, by the will of God and, in a sense, within the life of God. That God's relationship to man is not identical with man's relationship to man can be, therefore, in no doubt at all. But equally there seems to be no doubt that it is impossible for God to go beyond the exercise of 'influence' in His gracious dealing with man without departing from His own terms in the creation of the soul with which He is dealing. The limits of His influence we cannot determine: but, great as His influence undoubtedly is, influence it remains, and neither constraint nor automatic change.

CHAPTER III

PREDESTINATING GRACE

So far we have briefly surveyed the history of the formulation of the doctrine of grace, and we have sought to gain a general idea of what grace does and of what grace is. We are now in a position to begin the investigation of the various problems that arise in connection with this doctrine. They are all closely inter-related, so that it will be impossible to avoid some measure of overlapping when they are set out for separate examination: but the attempt to make an independent study of each of them ought to conduce to clearness of apprehension.

The first problem is the vindication of the God of love, who has been misrepresented as an arbitrary ruler bestowing His grace upon a favoured few, and deliberately consigning the rest of mankind to destruction. The doctrine of Predestinating Grace, as it is called, demands examination before any other matter is considered, if only because, in the minds of very many people, it constitutes so serious an offence as to prejudice them against any further consideration of the doctrine of grace.

Starting from the New Testament we find St. Paul proclaiming that "To them that love God all things work together for good, even to them that are called according to his purpose. For whom he foreknew, he also foreordained to be conformed to the image of his Son, that he might be the firstborn among many brethren: and whom he foreordained, them he also called: and whom he called, them he also justified: and whom he justified, them he also glorified." (Rom. viii. 28–30.) A little further on he asks, " What if God, willing to show his wrath, and to make his power known, endured with much long-suffering vessels of wrath fitted unto destruction: and that he might make known the riches of his glory upon vessels of mercy, which he afore prepared unto glory, even us, whom he also called, not from the Jews only, but also from the Gentiles? "

St. Augustine claimed to do no more than to reproduce what St. Paul had taught by revelation.

" I simply hold, indeed," he wrote, " what I see the apostle has most plainly taught us, that owing to one man all pass into condemnation who are born of Adam, unless they are born again in Christ, even as He has appointed them to be regenerated before they die in the body; having predestinated them to everlasting life as the most merciful bestower of grace; whilst to those whom He has predestinated to eternal death, He is also the most righteous awarder of punishment, not only on account of the sins which they add in the indulgence of their own will, but also because of their original sin, even if, as in the case of infants, they add nothing thereto."[1]

[1] *On the Soul and its Origin*, IV. 16.

This predestination of certain souls to eternal life is not, according to St. Augustine, a continuing process by which their number is increased with the increase of the human family. On the contrary, God has determined it once for all; and the number which He has fixed can never be altered. Their number, he says, is "so certain, that one can neither be added to them nor taken from them". "The number of the elect is certain, and neither to be increased nor diminished." [1]

The same belief was held by St. Anselm, who thus expressed it in his treatise *Why was God made Man?* "It cannot be doubted but that the rational nature which either is blessed, or to be blessed, with the contemplation of God, was foreknown by God to consist in a certain right and perfect number of individuals, so that this number may not rightly be either more or less. For either God knoweth not of what number they should consist, which is false, or He fixes it at that number which He sees to be most suitable. Wherefore those angels who fell were either made for the purpose of being of that number, or, because being beyond the number, they could not persevere, they of necessity fell, which it is absurd to suppose. Wherefore then, since they were made to be so many in number, either that number is to be made up as a matter of necessity, or that rational nature will exist in an imperfect number of individuals, which was foreknown

[1] *On Rebuke and Grace*, 39.

D

to be in a perfect one: which cannot be. Then it is
necessary that they should be replaced from humanity,
since there is no other nature whence they can be
replaced." (*c.* 16.)

Thus it came about, he contended, that " God
proposed to replace the number of angels who had
fallen, from that humanity which He had created
sinless."

The explanation which was offered by St. Thomas
Aquinas in defence of the belief in ' double predestination ' runs as follows:

" The reason for the predestination of some, and the
reprobation of others, must be sought for in the goodness of God. Thus He is said to have made all things
through His goodness, so that the divine goodness
might be represented in things. Now it is necessary
that God's goodness, which in itself is one and un-
divided, should be manifested in many ways in His
creation; because creatures in themselves cannot attain
to the simplicity of God. Thus it is that for the completion of the universe there are required different
grades of being; some of which hold a high and some
a low place in the universe. That the multiformity of
grades may be preserved in things, God allows some
evils, lest many good things should never happen. . . .
Let us then consider the whole of the human race, as
we consider the whole universe. God wills to manifest
His goodness in men; in respect of those whom He
predestines, by means of His mercy, in sparing them;
and in respect of others, whom He reprobates, by

means of His justice, in punishing them. This is the reason why God elects some and rejects others." [1]

Among the Protestant Reformers Luther gradually relaxed his hold on the doctrine of predestination, and he deprecated the undue attention which was being given to it by some of his followers; Zwingli whole-heartedly accepted it, believing that infants who died without sin, and virtuous pagans also, were to be reckoned among those whom God had predestinated to glory; and Calvin gave to the doctrine the clearest and most emphatic expression it has ever received, making it an essential article of faith in the system which he based upon belief in the absolute sovereignty of God. In his *Institutes of the Christian Religion*[2] Calvin declared his mind thus:

" Predestination we call the eternal decree of God by which He hath determined in Himself what He would have to become of every individual of mankind. For they are not all created with a similar destiny; but eternal life is foreordained for some, and eternal damnation for others. Every man, therefore, being created for one or other of these ends, we say he is predestinated either to life or to death." And again: " In conformity, therefore, with the clear doctrine of the Scriptures, we assert that, by an eternal and im-mutable counsel, God hath once for all determined both whom He would admit to salvation and whom He would condemn to destruction. We affirm that this counsel, as far as concerns the elect, is founded on

[1] *Summa*, I. Q. 23, Art. 5.   [2] III. xxi; 5, and xxii. 7,

His gratuitous mercy, totally irrespective of human merit: but that to those whom He devotes to condemnation, the gate of life is closed by a just and irreprehensible, but incomprehensible, judgment."

This series of quotations may be concluded by an extract from the *Westminster Confession of Faith*.[1] Here it is stated that:

" All those whom God hath predestinated unto life, and those only, He is pleased, in His appointed and accepted time, effectually to call, by His word and Spirit, out of that state of sin and death in which they are by nature, to grace and salvation by Jesus Christ; enlightening their minds spiritually and savingly to understand the things of God; taking away their heart of stone, and giving unto them an heart of flesh, renewing their wills, and by His almighty power determining them to that which is good; and effectually drawing them to Jesus Christ; yet so as they come most freely, being made willing by His grace. This effectual call is of God's free and special grace alone, not from anything at all foreseen in man; who is altogether passive therein, until, being quickened and renewed by the Holy Spirit, he is thereby enabled to answer this call, and to embrace the grace offered and conveyed in it. Elect infants, dying in infancy, are regenerated and saved by Christ through the Spirit, who worketh when, and where, and how He pleaseth. So also are all other elect persons, who are incapable of being outwardly called by the ministry of the word.

[1] Chap. x

Others not elected, although they may be called by the ministry of the word, and may have some common operations of the Spirit, yet they never truly come unto Christ, and therefore cannot be saved: much less can men not professing the Christian religion be saved in any other way whatsoever, be they ever so diligent to frame their lives according to the light of nature, and the law of that religion they do profess; and to assert and maintain that they may, is very pernicious, and to be detested."

There is no doubt that views such as these are highly offensive to what is called ' the modern mind '. They seem to present us with an arbitrary and cruel God who is utterly irreconcilable with the God of love; and, when present-day critics dismiss these views as ' perfectly horrible ', they not infrequently add an expression of their complete inability to understand how people ever came to hold them. It may be well, therefore, to inquire into the answer to that question. How did sincere and very able Christian thinkers come to believe that the doctrine of predestination is a necessary part of the Faith? That they did honestly think so, the quotations given above make it impossible to doubt. How did their mistake arise—for the conviction that it is a mistake is very strong—and, when they published it to the Christian world, were they themselves happy about it, and did other people raise no protest?

The explanation of their formulation of the doctrine would appear to lie partly in their own experience and their reflection upon it, partly in their observation of the lives of others, and partly in their study of Biblical theology and of philosophy. In some cases they were men who had been ' born again ' by an unforgettable experience of conversion. St. Paul had been delivered from intellectual error and from the insupportable burden, as he knew it to be when he looked back, of a legalistic system; St. Augustine had been emancipated from bondage to evil living; and both men knew before all else that their deliverance was due, not to anything in themselves, but to the mercy of God alone. They had not only done nothing to deserve the great mercy shown to them; they had fought against it to the uttermost. And yet God had claimed them for His own, because, as they believed, He had set His love upon them, and for no other reason. Other men, who had not known the intense experience of such particular and miraculous invasion of divine power in their lives, were yet so deeply conscious of an overruling providence in all their ways that they were constrained to think and to speak as St. Paul and St. Augustine had done, the testimony of those two saints no doubt assisting their convictions. God had made it abundantly clear that they were His chosen servants, and they did not hesitate to proclaim the fact, out of their gratitude and as an expression of their devotion.

Then these men looked out upon the world around them, and marked the great difference to be seen in the lives of so many others. Whatever their age and generation they saw plainly the accumulated tokens

of the destructive power of evil in the lives of men,
and of the utter helplessness of men who were caught
in its toils; for, though the signs are more abundant,
more horrible, and more strident, in some ages than in
others, in no age are they wanting. Individuals and
groups alike provide an unbroken succession of demonstrations of sudden and inexplicable moral failures,
lapses, and perversions, of moral outrages revealing
unsuspected depths of turpitude, of disaster overtaking
honest effort which seemed to be fully deserving of
success, and of the triumph of deceit and roguery in a
world condemned to suffer by the results of its own
blind awards; and all these things declared to such
observers the inevitability of failure and disaster where
God has not chosen to bestow His favour. Their feeling is exactly expressed by the oft-quoted words:
" There but for the grace of God goes John Bradford."

Turning to their Bibles for an explanation of the
large element of tragedy in life, and for the confirmation of their faith in their own deliverance, these men
were naturally drawn to the attentive study of the
story of the sin of Adam, and to the teaching of St.
Paul concerning the Second Adam and " the grace of
the Lord Jesus Christ ". If, as they believed, Adam
and Eve were truly the first parents of the human race,
and if their sin, man's primal sin, truly produced the
results which are recorded in the Book of Genesis, then
it would appear to be inevitable that they should find
in the sin of Adam and Eve the cause and the justification of all man's tribulations and of his inability to

enjoy communion with God. It would seem to them that men had forfeited all claim on God, and were an accursed race. If they asked themselves why God should continue to suffer man's existence, why He did not bring the human race to an end, again the Bible provided them with an answer. God's grace had determined that, though He was under no kind of obligation to any man, yet He would deliver some; and this deliverance He had accomplished by the Incarnation of Jesus Christ. To His incarnate Son God had given certain souls, to be retrieved by Him as brands from the burning, and these souls were brought to the hearing and acceptance of the Gospel of Jesus Christ by the providential ordering of the circumstances of their lives. Those who were left could not reasonably complain; for they suffered the due consequences of their corporate sin, which was committed by man's original parents and, in them, by the whole human family. Those who were taken, on the contrary, had every reason to bless God for the undeserved mercy which His grace had bestowed upon them.

The many questions which must arise in the minds of those who read this summary explanation of the grounds on which the doctrine of predestination has been held must be considered presently. At this stage let us remember that men tend to find what they want when they turn to literature in quest of support for opinions which they have already formed. There is, of course, very much in the Bible that might have given pause to those who found only rigid predestin-

arianism there: but their bitter remembrance of the
past, and their exalted consciousness of privilege in the
present, led them to find and to stress all that bore on
the side of the case to which they were so strongly predisposed. Furthermore, they considered the subject
against a background of philosophy and were well
acquainted with the insoluble problem of man's free
will. How can the Creator, from whom all life proceeds and by whom it is maintained, create utterly
dependent and yet truly free creatures? These men
had wrestled with this problem, and they knew much
more about its difficulties than many of those who
would lightly dismiss their teaching as foolish. Predestination seemed to them to be the only possible conclusion which did not derogate from the sovereignty of
God; and they were strong in their possession of a
faith which, as it seemed to them, tallied with human
experience, with the divine revelation which was
recorded in the Scriptures, and with a sound
philosophy.

Were they at all subjected to criticism by any who
felt as ' the modern mind ' feels about it; and were
they themselves at all disturbed by their conclusions,
seeing that these involved the destruction of the great
majority of their contemporaries? Certainly they were
much criticised; and sometimes perhaps their answers
suggest that they were not altogether easy in their
minds, though reservation must be made in the case of
Calvin and many of his followers.

Objection to the idea of divine reprobation was very

strongly expressed by John Cassian, who wrote as follows: " He whose will it is that not one of these little ones should perish—how without monstrous sacrilege shall it be thought that He does not will all men to be saved, but merely some in place of all? " (*Coll.* xiii. 7.) St. Augustine's uneasiness was betrayed by a certain degree of unwillingness to lay at God's door the charge of predestinating any to destruction. Though expressions of this belief may be found in his writings, he may be fairly said to have taught ' preterition ' or ' pretermission ' rather than ' reprobation '. That is to say, he affirmed that those who were predestined to glory received at God's hands an entirely undeserved mercy, while those who were not chosen for this gracious treatment simply suffered what man's sin had brought upon them, by the exercise of righteous judgment. God was not responsible for their loss. But because Augustine was faced with the fact that some who appeared to be numbered among the elect relapsed into sin, and probably also because he grasped gladly at an opportunity of enlarging the operation of God's grace and thus of weakening the force of the argument used by his critics, he devised a distinction between ' sufficient grace ' and ' efficacious grace ', both of which were to be recognised as the grace of justification. Out of the whole mass of mankind, doomed to destruction because of sin, God chooses some to be the recipients of ' sufficient grace ', by which their feet are to be set in the way of salvation. But of these only a part will ever arrive—that

part to which God adds, as a supplement to the ' sufficient grace ' already bestowed, the further gift of ' efficacious grace '. Those to whom this second gift is
denied will fall away; the others will persevere. Mankind is thus to be divided into three parts: those who
will ultimately be saved; those who will be associated
with them for a time, but will ultimately fall away;
and those for whom there is no hope of salvation at
any time. As to which it may be said that St.
Augustine's ingenuity not only lends no help to a
troubled mind, but is calculated rather to increase the
sense of resentment against arbitrary action by adding
to it a semblance of horrible cunning.

To most minds it will seem, no doubt, that there is
really no difference between ' preterition ' and ' reprobation ', even if we start with the assumption that all
men deserve destruction. If God selects from the mass
some who are to be saved, purely as an act of grace
and without reference to desert, He cannot escape responsibility for the rejection of the others. For, since
He is God, it cannot be that His grace is limited, so
that it is exhausted after a certain number of men have
received it; nor can it be that God has so contrived the
universe that He is precluded from diminishing the
total number of men or, alternatively, from increasing
the number of the elect. By omitting to deliver, God
must be held in effect to condemn. As Calvin pointed
out, with his customary directness, " Many indeed, as
if they would avert odium from God, acknowledge
election in such a way as to deny that anyone is repro-

bated, but altogether absurdly and childishly, since election would not stand unless it were opposed to reprobation. God is said to separate those whom He adopts to salvation; to say that others obtain by chance, or acquire by their own industry, that which election alone confers on a few would be worse than absurd. Those, therefore, whom God passes over He reprobates, and that from no other cause than that He wills to exclude them from the inheritance which He predestinates for His sons."[1] Wesley made protest with an equal directness in *A Sermon on Free Grace*, though he wrote from a completely different standpoint. " Call it therefore by whatever name you please, election, preterition, predestination, or reprobation, it comes in the end to the irresistible decree of God, one part of mankind are infallibly saved, and the rest infallibly damned; it is impossible that any of the former should be damned, or that any of the latter should be saved."

Another attempt to deliver God from the responsibility of assigning large numbers of His creatures to destruction is found in the assertion that He elects to life only those whose good deeds He foresees. The rest are condemned because God knows beforehand that they will deserve to be condemned. This is known as the doctrine of Predestination on the Ground of Foreseen Merits (*Praedestinatio post praevisa merita*, or *ex praevisis meritis*). It was widely held before St. Augustine's day, and he himself was at first disposed to accept it: but on consideration he turned away from

[1] *Institutes,* III. xxiii. 1.

it and, in his conflict with the Massilian school, showed himself to be strongly antagonistic to the view, which those theologians held. As Calvin said,[1] "Ambrose, Origen, and Jerome believed that God dispenses His grace among men according to His foreknowledge of the good use which every individual will make of it. Augustine also was once of the same sentiment; but when he had made a greater proficiency in scriptural knowledge, he not only retracted, but powerfully confuted it."

St. Augustine believed, of course, in the divine foreknowledge of all that happens in time: but he contended that foreknowledge is to be distinguished from predetermination, and that it is not to be accounted in any sense as the ground of predestination. God's prevision of what a man will do cannot be said to constrain that man to act accordingly, St. Augustine declared, basing his answer to a problem of extreme difficulty on an invalid analogy between the foreknowledge of God and a man's foreknowledge of another man's action. And further, apart from all question of the divine constraint of the human will, he asserted that it is utterly false to suppose that man can merit salvation by right conduct and that God merely recognises this in advance by predestinating to glory those who will subsequently earn that state. In his treatise *On the Predestination of the Saints* (*c.* 34) he writes, "What is it that the apostle says, 'As he hath chosen us in himself before the foundation of

[1] *Institutes*, III. xxii. 8.

the world'? And assuredly, if this were said because God foreknew that they would believe, not because He Himself would make them believers, the Son is speaking against such a foreknowledge as that when He says, 'Ye have not chosen me, but I have chosen you'; when God should rather have foreknown this very thing that they themselves would have chosen Him, so that they might deserve to be chosen by Him. Therefore they were elected before the foundation of the world with that predestination in which God foreknew what He Himself would do; but they were elected out of the world with that calling whereby God fulfilled that which He predestinated."

The Franciscan schoolmen followed the Massilians in the view that God does discriminate between the elect and the reprobate on the basis of His foreknowledge of their deeds; and they cleverly combined this opinion with the Augustinian view by introducing the distinction between 'efficient cause' and 'ground'. "The cause of election," Alexander of Hales said, "is on the side of God and not on ours: but the ground of election may be on the side of man, in accordance with the co-operation of his free will." John Scotus pointed out, as a sufficient explanation of the matter, that God is not in the time-process, and that we ought to think of Him, therefore, not as predestinating the issues of life before time began, but as continuously determining them as every man's Great Contemporary.

St. Thomas Aquinas would not allow that God's foreknowledge of man's merit was the cause of predestination: but he showed that the matter inevitably presents different aspects when it is viewed from God's side and from man's. " The effect of predestination may be considered in a twofold light. In one way, it may be considered in particular; and thus there is no reason why one effect of predestination should not be the reason or cause of another, a subsequent effect being the reason of a previous effect, as its final cause, and the previous effect being the reason of the subsequent as its meritorious cause, which is reduced to the disposition of the matter. Thus we might say that God pre-ordained to give glory on account of merit, and that He pre-ordained to give grace to merit glory. In another way, the effect of predestination may be considered in general. Thus, it is impossible that the whole of the effect of predestination in general should have any cause as coming from us; because whatsoever is in man disposing him towards salvation, is all included under the effect of predestination; even the preparation for grace. For neither does this happen otherwise than by divine help, according to the prophet Jeremiah (Lam. v. 21): ' Turn Thou us unto Thee, O Lord, and we shall be turned.' Yet predestination has in this way, in regard to its effect, the goodness of God for its reason; towards which the whole effect of pre-destination is directed as to an end; and from which it proceeds, as from its first moving principle."[1]

Calvin was in complete agreement with St. Augustine as to the absolute nature of predestination, and he

[1] *Summa*, 1. Q. 23, Art. 5.

would allow no mitigation of the doctrine. He noted that " Predestination, by which God adopts some to the hope of life, and adjudges others to eternal death, no one desirous of the credit of piety dares absolutely to deny. But it is involved in many cavils, especially by those who make foreknowledge the cause of it. We maintain that both belong to God; but it is preposterous to represent one as dependent on the other." [1] The attempt made by the schoolmen to combine the two points of view was emphatically dismissed by him. " We shall not dwell," he wrote, " upon the sophistry of Thomas Aquinas, that the foreknowledge of merits is not the cause of predestination in regard to the act of him who predestinates; but that with regard to us it may in some sense be so called, according to the particular consideration of predestination: as when God is said to predestinate glory for man according to merits, because He decreed to give him grace, by which glory is merited. For, since the Lord allows us to contemplate nothing in election but His mere goodness, the desire of anyone to see anything more is a preposterous disposition. But, if we were inclined to a contention of subtlety, we should be at no loss to refute this petty sophism of Aquinas. He contends that glory is in a certain sense predestinated for the elect according to their merits, because God predestinates to them the grace by which glory is merited. What if I, on the contrary, reply that predestination is subordinate to election to life, and attendant upon it; that grace is pre-

[1] *Institutes*, III. xxi. 5.

destinated to those to whom the possession of glory
has been already assigned, because it pleases the Lord
to conduct His children from election to justification?
For hence it will follow that predestination to glory is
rather the cause of predestination to grace, than the
contrary. But let us dismiss these controversies. They
are unnecessary with those who think they have
wisdom enough in the word of God. For it was truly
remarked by an ancient ecclesiastical writer that ' They
who ascribe God's election to merits are wiser than
they ought to be!' "[1]   And he refers to a certain
"Valla, a man otherwise not much versed in
theology", who appeared to him to have given evidence of "a superior acuteness and judiciousness by
showing that this controversy is unnecessary, because
both life and death are acts of God's will rather than
of His foreknowledge. If God simply foresaw the
fates of men and did not also dispose and fix them by
His determination, there would be room to agitate the
question whether His providence or foresight rendered
them at all necessary. But since He foresees future
events only in consequence of His decree that they shall
happen, it is useless to contend about foreknowledge,
while it is evident that all things come to pass rather
by ordination and decree."[2]

One particular point in this debate concerning the
relation between prevision and predestination divided
the disputants subsequently into Supra-lapsarians and

[1] *Institutes*, III. xxii. 9.
[2] *Institutes*, III. xxiii. 6.

E

Infra- or Sub-lapsarians. The former held, with Calvin and Beza, that divine predestination preceded the Fall, which was included within its scope and provided the field for the operation of grace. The latter held that predestination followed upon the divine prevision of the Fall, which constituted an appeal to God's grace. Calvin had written, " Let no one murmur that God might have made a better provision for our safety by preventing the Fall of Adam. For such an objection ought to be abominated, as too presumptuously curious, by all pious minds; and it belongs also to the mystery of predestination."[1] And he gave this answer to some who opposed the doctrine of predestination. " They further object, ' Were they not, by the decree of God, antecedently predestinated to that corruption which is now stated as the cause of condemnation? When they perish in their corruption, therefore, they only suffer the punishment of that misery into which, in consequence of his predestination, Adam fell, and precipitated his posterity with him. Is He not unjust, therefore, in treating His creatures with such cruel mockery? ' I confess, indeed, that all the descendants of Adam fell by the divine will into that miserable condition in which they are now involved."[2]

The contrary view was take by Arminius and his followers, who taught that predestination is in accordance with the divine prevision, and that there is therefore no ground for calling God's justice in ques-

[1] *Institutes*, II. i. 10.
[2] *Institutes*, III. xxiii. 4.

tion. To the declaration on this point which they included in the *Confession of the Remonstrants* (xvii. 3), " Calling is effectual from the result, rather than from the sole intention of God ", answer was returned by the Calvinists in the *Canons of Dort* (Arts. 9 and 10) that " This same election was made, not because there was foreseen faith, and obedience of faith, holiness, or any other good quality and disposition, as a cause or condition required before in the man to be elected; but election is unto faith, and obedience of faith, holiness, and every other good quality and disposition. But the cause of this free election is the good pleasure of God alone."

Doubtless the problem will continue to be debated until the end of time, with no prospect of arriving at a satisfactory and agreed conclusion. We are bound to believe in the divine omniscience; we are bound also to believe in the freedom of man's will, as will be argued in the next chapter. These are the terms of an antinomy, or opposition of thought, which completely baffles the human mind. But, so far as the doctrine of predestinating grace is concerned, it will be seen that those who teach that predestination is dependent upon God's foreknowledge of what men will do, in seeking to deliver God from the charge of arbitrary action, are, in effect, actually denying that there is any predestination at all, in the proper sense of the term. If prescience necessarily involves predetermination, as some philosophers think, their denial is invalidated, and the matter remains where it was before they made their suggestion for the relief of conscience. If prescience does not involve predetermination, as others think, then they have not only delivered God from the charge of injustice and greatly relieved men's consciences by abolishing the doctrine of predestination, but they have shown that the relationship between God and man is purely one of merit and reward, or of demerit and punishment, and they have reduced the doctrine of grace to the limits which were allowed by Pelagius.

The third and final position taken by those whose faith in predestination is challenged is an appeal to the fact that we are God's creatures, and a blank assertion that we have no right to question His action. We are reminded that St. Paul wrote: " Nay but, O man, who art thou that repliest against God? " (Rom. ix. 20). St. Augustine also, writing about God's influence on man's will, said: " Should any man be for constraining us to examine into that profound fact of our moral nature, why this person is so far advised as to be persuaded, and that person is not, there are only two thoughts occurring to me, which I should like to advance as my answer: ' O the depth of the riches! ' and ' Is there unrighteousness with God? ' If the man is displeased with such an answer he must seek more learned disputants. Let him beware, however, lest he find in them presumptuous wranglers."[1]

Similarly Calvin declared that " Foolish mortals enter into many contentions with God, as though they

On the Spirit and the Letter, c. 60.

could arraign Him to plead to their accusations. In the first place they inquire by what right the Lord is angry with His creatures who had not provoked Him by any previous offence; for that, to devote to destruction whom He pleases is more like the caprice of a tyrant than the lawful sentence of a judge; that men have reason, therefore, to expostulate with God if they are predestinated to eternal death without any demerit of their own, merely by His Sovereign will. If such thoughts ever enter the minds of pious men, they will be sufficiently enabled to break their violence by this one consideration, how exceedingly presumptuous it is only to inquire into the causes of the divine will, which is in fact, and is justly entitled to be, the cause of everything that exists. For, if it has any cause, then there must be something antecedent, on which it depends; which it is impious to suppose. For the will of God is the highest rule of justice; so that what He wills must be considered just, for this very reason, because he wills it. When it is inquired, therefore, why the Lord did so, the answer must be, Because He would."[1]

This attempt to break off the discussion cannot be accepted, however, as a satisfactory conclusion to the matter. A reverent agnosticism is becoming in all Christian inquirers; and only the merest novice in the ways of Christian thought will suppose that, if we continue to think with sufficient industry and ability, we may expect to arrive at the true solution of every

[1] *Institutes*, III. xxii. 2.

problem of life. Many things must be laid aside for the time being, after we have proceeded as far as our powers will allow us to go, in the hope and expectation of more light in another world. But to conclude this question of predestination with an ascription of presumption against those who seek to deliver God from a charge of tyranny and monstrous injustice will not do. Has not God committed to us the power of moral judgment, the power to appraise moral actions, as a necessary instrument of our own moral growth? And are we not bound to exercise this power for the vindication of God's honour? To leave the doctrine of predestination where Calvin left it is to admit such a discrepancy between the moral standards of God and those of man as to require us either to make a sustained protest against the ways of God or to abandon the Christian moral code as one that has no true foundation. As Aubrey Moore has said, " Calvinism is not accidentally but essentially immoral, since it makes the distinction between right and wrong a matter of positive enactment, and thereby makes it possible to assert that what is immoral for man is moral for God, because He is above morality."[1] If we are to continue to attach any importance to the Christian conscience, enlightened, as we believe, by the Holy Spirit of God, we must refuse to accept the doctrine of double predestination, and we are bound to try to discover what truth there is in the doctrine of the predestination or election of the elect, beginning with the conviction that

[1] *Science and the Faith,* p. 119.

there can be nothing in that truth which will require us to think of God as being ' above morality '.

Berdyaev has declared in his latest book[1] that " The Gospel does not recognise a race of the good who are going to heaven and a race of the wicked who are going to hell." This dictum admits of no contradiction. It is inconceivable that any unprejudiced and careful reader, examining the Gospels for the first time, should suppose that our Lord addressed Himself to a number of people, on the one hand, who were in possession of an indefectible goodness and an assurance of salvation, and, on the other hand, to a number of people who were quite incapable of moral and spiritual restoration, and consequently were moving forward to inescapable condemnation and irreparable loss. The Psalmist's conviction that " The Lord is loving unto every man: and His mercy is over all His works " was established beyond all doubt by the reiterated assurance of the divine Fatherhood which was given by the incarnate Son, and by His unceasing appeal to sinners to turn to Him and to walk in the light of His love. There is no doubt whatever about His discrimination between penitent and unrepentant sinners, and between the joy of the redeemed and the pain of those who are cast out: but there is equally no doubt that our Lord does not contemplate for one moment the division of mankind into " a race of the good " and " a race of the wicked ". If " many are called, but few are chosen ", it is clear that, while the calling is

[1] *The Destiny of Man*, p. 145.

of God alone, the limitations of the final adoption are imposed upon God by man's failure to strive towards the heights of his vocation.

While, however, it is unquestionably true that God " willeth that all men should be saved, and come to the knowledge of the truth " (1 Tim. ii. 4), there is obviously a great diversity in the gifts with which men are endowed and in the circumstances and opportunities of their lives, and this raises the question of election, in the sense that some are chosen to be God's agents for the furtherance of His purposes for mankind at large. Thus it would seem to be necessary, first of all, to accept the position that all who have been incorporated into the Church are, as St. Peter called them, " an elect race " (1 Peter ii. 9). Remembering that they are described also as " a royal priesthood ", we cannot fail to recognise the true nature and purpose of their election. To them is committed the priestly activity of prayer on behalf of all sorts and conditions of men, and to them is entrusted the saving Gospel of the Lord Jesus Christ for communication to those who are yet in darkness. They are ' elect ' for God's service. If they fail Him, their own salvation is jeopardised but God's purposes are not frustrated. His resources are unlimited and His love is unfailing. His Spirit is at work in the hearts of all men everywhere; and He will judge, not according to the failure of His human agents, but according to the use His children make of the knowledge and the gifts and the opportunities which have been bestowed upon them. This truth was most strikingly set out by a seventeenth-century writer whose teaching is summarized by von Hügel.[1] " I believe," the latter says, " the true scheme, as concerns religion, to have been best developed by Cardinal Juan de Lugo, the Spanish Jesuit, who wrote in Rome under the eyes of Pope Urban VIII, at the end of the seventeenth century. De Lugo first lays down that, according to Catholic doctrine, God gives light, sufficient for its salvation, to every soul that attains to the use of reason in this life. He next asks, What is the ordinary method by which God offers and renders possible this salvation? And he answers that, though God doubtless can work moral miracles, these do not appear to be the rule, and are not in strictness necessary; that the human soul, in all times and places, has a certain natural affinity for, and need of, truth; and again, that the various philosophical schools and religious bodies throughout mankind all contain and hand down, amid various degrees of human error and distortion, *some truth*, some gleams and elements of divine truth. Now what happens as a rule is simply this: the soul that in good faith seeks God, His truth and love, concentrates its attention, under the influence of grace, upon these elements of truth be they many or few, which are offered to it in the sacred books and religious schools and assemblies of the Church, Sect, or Philosophy in which it has been brought up. It feeds upon these elements, the others are simply passed by; and

[1] *Essays and Addresses*, I. 252f.

divine grace, under cover of these elements, feeds and saves this soul. I submit that this view admirably combines a sense of man's profound need of tradition, institution, training, with full justice to the importance of the dispositions and acts of the individual soul, and, above all, with a keen sense of the need of special graces offered by God to the several souls. And such a view in no way levels down or damps the missionary ardour. Buddhism does not become equal to Mohammedanism, nor Mohammedanism to Judaism, nor Platonism to Christianity, nor Socinianism, or even Lutheranism, to Catholicism. It merely claims that everywhere there is *some* truth; that this truth comes originally from God; and that this truth, great or little, is usually mediated to the soul, neither by a spiritual miracle nor by the sheer efforts of individuals, but by traditions, schools, and churches. We thus attain an outlook, generous, rich, elastic; yet also graduated, positive, unitary and truly Catholic." It would seem to be impossible to state the matter more truly and more convincingly.

Further, it is evident that among those who constitute the 'elect race', which is 'a royal priesthood', there is a great diversity of gifts, vocations, and offices, suggesting a supplementary election to peculiar service for the edification of the whole Body of the children of grace. Some are called to the ministry of administrative leadership and pastoral care; some are called to the ministry of teaching and inspiration; some are called to the ministry of succour and healing; some are called to the ministry of the stewardship of material possessions. And in each and every way of calling there is a kind of predestinating grace to be discerned, planning and guiding without constraining, providing opportunities for the exercise of the divinely appointed ministry, together with the necessary gifts for the same and the stimulation of the will to use them, and advancing towards its perfection the soul that is called, by means of the response which it makes to its vocation. But this involves no suggestion of the rejection of the poor, the simple, the 'ordinary members' of the Body. Rather is it for their sake that the others are specially endowed, and called to be fellow-workers with Christ, that they may be used by Him in the accomplishment of His desire to bring "many sons unto glory".

CHAPTER IV

GRACE, PREVENIENT AND SUBSEQUENT

Two familiar Collects will serve to suggest the nature of the problem with which we are now to deal. The first is the prayer which is prescribed for use during the last week of the Church's Year: " Stir up, we beseech thee, O Lord, the wills of thy faithful people; that they, plenteously bringing forth the fruits of good works, may of thee be plenteously rewarded; through Jesus Christ our Lord." In this prayer there is an assumption and an appeal. The assumption is that will-power is possessed by the Faithful; the appeal is for grace to set in motion the will to good. The second Collect carries us beyond this, and explicitly introduces the subject-matter of this chapter. " Prevent us, O Lord, in all our doings," it runs, " with thy most gracious favour, and further us with thy continual help; that in all our works, begun, continued, and ended in thee, we may glorify thy holy name, and finally by thy mercy obtain everlasting life; through Jesus Christ our Lord." Here is the same suggestion of the necessity of divine assistance for the stimulation and direction of our wills: but there is also a petition for an additional aid, so that the stirring of our will to good may actually issue in good works.

Two stages are thus marked out in that operation of grace whereby we are persuaded and assisted to the discharge of our bounden duty. First, God prepares us to a right disposition, by the bestowal of prevenient grace, which puts into our minds good desires and moves us to the point of determining to give effect to them. Then He adds subsequent grace, to enable us to carry out our purpose.

The many controversies which have gathered round this matter of grace, prevenient and subsequent, are concerned with the question of man's ability to co-operate, at any stage and in any degree, with the divine action. Attention has been specially directed, in these debates, to the process of man's return to God; and, although the two prayers which have been quoted are concerned with the needs of those who have already been claimed by God as His elect, we must also bear in mind the case of the unconverted, and inquire into the validity of belief in the operation of this twofold bestowal of grace in connection with their redemption from the world. The doctrine of predestination, which we considered in the previous chapter, is clearly bound up with the idea of the complete inability of man to play any part in his own conversion; and if it should indeed be found that, when God calls a man, he himself has no power to determine his response, it would be necessary to repudiate the finding of the previous chapter and to accept the doctrine of double pre-destination. Grace, prevenient and subsequent, be-stowed upon an unconverted man, would be exactly equivalent to predestinating grace; and those to whom prevenient grace was denied would be predestinated to condemnation and death.

It will be evident that, in respect both of the converted and of the unconverted, the question of man's ability to co-operate with divine grace presents us, on the philosophical side, with the insoluble problem of free will; while on the theological side it is closely associated with the doctrine of the Fall of man. Our estimate of man's capacity for the reception and the use of the Grace of God must depend upon our conception of the damage which resulted to human nature from the Fall, if we assume for the moment that something in the nature of what is commonly called ' the Fall ' actually took place. As an example of what is meant we may quote the terms of the ninth of the Thirty-nine Articles. " The condition of man after the fall of Adam is such, that he cannot turn and prepare himself, by his own natural strength and good works, to faith and calling upon God. Wherefore we have no power to do good works pleasant and acceptable to God, without the grace of God by Christ preventing us that we may have a good will, and working with us when we have that good will."

The doctrine of the Fall expounds the Christian belief that human nature, as it came originally from the hands of God, was better than the human nature whose frailty is universally declared in history and in present experience, and that the deterioration was effected in the very earliest days of the history of mankind, by man's own action. It is commonly but erroneously supposed that the doctrine is altogether dependent upon the acceptance of the Genesis story of Adam and Eve as an exact record of an historical event. While, however, it is true that the great majority of Christians in the past have so received the Scripture, and that many still do so to-day, the doctrine of the Fall of man is in no way invalidated if the findings of modern criticism are accepted, and the Genesis story is recognised as an allegorical presentation of the truth. The conjectural reconstruction of unspoiled human nature in terms of the status and privilege supposedly enjoyed by Adam and Eve before their commission of the primal sin may well appear to be merely fanciful and quite irrelevant when they are put before the convinced believer in man's evolution from the lower animal creation. He is eager to set a brutish conception of cave-dwelling primitive man over against the theological presentation of the first parents of the human race walking with God in the Garden of Eden, and to claim that the truth lies entirely on his side and only false imagination on the other. He proceeds to explain all the present irregularities of man's life as a consequence of the persistence in him of certain animal characteristics, and to contend that, in his upward progress, man is gradually eliminating these or reducing them to order. In place of a Fall and a subsequent state of degradation he insists upon the recognition of progressive achievement and of a steady rise away from the level of animal life. But the facts are against him—the facts, namely, of a range of wrongdoing which far exceeds anything that can be reasonably attributed to animal instinct alone; of the continuing association of deep-seated and undiminished sinfulness with advanced culture and a show of good manners; and the abiding sense of inability and frustration which possesses all who strive towards the fulfilment of the moral ideals which they have inherited or conceived.

From time to time theologians have speculated about the possibility of a pre-mundane Fall, in order to account for the fact that disorder and death had declared themselves in the world before man's arrival on the scene, and as a result of their recognition of diabolical agency in the dissemination of evil. It must be said that something of the kind seems to be demanded by what is now known of the process of evolution. What appears to the scientist to be the halting and unnecessarily prolonged experimentation of Nature, with its many mistakes and prodigal rejections and its persistent achievement in spite of them all, may well be explained by the theological hypothesis of a ' Fall ' before the world began to be. But the conception of an opposition to the Creator at such an early stage, however true it may be in fact, would seem to admit of no more than a mythological presentation to human minds, and to be exceedingly vulnerable to criticism as being a matter of pure speculation. Moreover, unless he is prepared to abandon completely the Christian doctrine of man, it is not permissible for the theo-

logian to advance the theory of a pre-mundane Fall
as an answer to the scientific criticism of the doctrine
of the Fall of man, and as a substitute for that doctrine. He is not free to minimise the gap between man
and the animal world, and to surrender the inherent
dignity and responsibility of human nature. From the
moment when that nature is constituted, by whatever
means, it is impossible to regard man as merely a
superior animal. He belongs to another order; and,
while he is obviously exposed to the attack of whatever evil agencies and influences may be operating in
the world as the result of a pre-mundane Fall, it is
clear that any injury resulting to him from their action
cannot be credited entirely to them, so as to represent
man as the helpless animal victim of heredity and
circumstances. Man is by nature such—his present
nature leaves it in no doubt—that his reactions to
constraining forces within and without must always
be taken into account. He can himself be his greatest
enemy; and it would appear that he adopted this *rôle*
at a very early stage in his history. A pre-mundane
Fall there may well have been: but the evidence for a
Fall of man is even more convincing.

If many generations of Christians have been wrong
in believing that Adam and Eve were actual persons, it
is good that we should now be able to correct their
mistake. It is much more important, however, that at
the same time we should hold fast to the truth which
was bound up with their delusion. This requires us
not merely to regard Adam and Eve as Everyman and

his wife, and to find in their story an allegorical representation of the entrance of sin into every human life, but also to recognise that mankind is a family, that it has a bad family history, that its bad record began very early in its career, and that its badness lies not in its failure to eliminate rapidly the marks of its animal origin but in its perverted use of the endowment which was expressly bestowed upon it when it began to exist as something essentially different from the merely animal world. The sin of Adam and Eve signifies the initial act of sin by which the human family, departing from the dictates of conscience, began to corrupt the nature which was bestowed upon it by its Creator, and embarked upon a career of corporate and individual alienation from the mind and purpose of God. If we would place ourselves in a position to appreciate the operation of grace upon perverted human nature, we are clearly under the necessity of considering the extent of man's loss through his earliest sin, and the enduring resultant of the self-injury which he inflicted.

Rejecting the opinion of Pelagius, who held that the descendants of Adam and Eve were not involved in any of the consequences of the primal sin, theologians have speculated freely about the nature of Adam before the Fall and about the changes that were effected in the human nature shared by him and all his offspring, as a result of the Fall. They are agreed that mankind has fallen from a higher estate to a lower, and that human nature has suffered injury and loss: but they differ widely in their analysis of the original constitution of human nature, and in their calculation of the extent of the Fall and the degree of the damage which was inflicted by it. On a very broad and general classification it may be said that there are theories of privation, of depravity, and of complete depravity. Special gifts enjoyed by Adam before the Fall were withdrawn from man because of his sin, so that normal human nature remained, deprived only of its super-endowment, or to some extent disordered by the deprivation; or the true human nature, which existed with or without any supplementary gifts before the Fall, was very seriously injured and degraded as a result of the Fall; or again, the true human nature which belonged to Adam before he sinned was rendered wholly corrupt by the Fall. According to all three types of theory the loss and the damage resulting from the sin of Adam are transmitted to the whole human family as ' Original Sin ', a phrase which is to be understood to mean ' inherited sinfulness ', most commonly with the idea also of ' transmitted guilt '.

The doctrine of total depravity, or of the complete corruption of human nature, is particularly associated with the Protestant Reformers, Luther and Calvin, the latter in this case being rather less positive than the former. Luther in the *Augsburg Confession*, and Melanchthon in his *Apology*, which he wrote in explanation of the *Confession*, taught that Adam's sin resulted in the utter degradation of human nature, and consequently in the guilt of the human family by reason of its possession of a nature which is an offence to God. An official document of the Lutheran Church, known as the *Formulary of Concord* (1577), affirmed not only that " original sin in human nature is not merely the total lack or defect of virtuous powers in spiritual things which pertain unto God; but also that into the place of the image of God which has been lost there has succeeded an intimate, grievous, most profound and abyss-like, inscrutable and indescribable corruption of the whole nature and of all the powers of man, most chiefly of the superior and principal faculties of the soul, a corruption which infects the mind, intellect, heart, and will. Wherefore after the Fall man receives from his parents by heredity a congenitally depraved impulse, filthiness of heart, depraved concupiscences and depraved inclinations." (i, 11.) Apart from a few hesitations in connection with the problem of pagan virtues, Calvin took the same general view of the condition of man in consequence of the Fall, and stated it in equally unmistakable terms. " These two things, therefore," he wrote,[1] " should be distinctly observed: first, that our nature being so totally vitiated and depraved, we are, on account of this very corruption, considered as convicted and justly condemned in the sight of God, to whom nothing is acceptable but righteousness, innocence, and purity. . . . The other thing to be remarked is that this depravity never ceases in us, but is perpetually producing new fruits, those works of the flesh which we have before described, like the emission of

[1] *Institutes*, ii, i, 8.

flame and sparks from a heated furnace; or like the streams of water from a never-failing spring. Wherefore, those who have defined original sin as a privation of the original righteousness, which we ought to possess, though they comprise the whole of the subject, yet have not used language sufficiently expressive of its operation and influence. For our nature is not only destitute of all good, but is so fertile in all evils that it cannot remain inactive. Those who have called it 'concupiscence' have used an expression not improper, if it were only added, which is far from being conceded by most persons, that everything in man, the understanding and will, the soul and body, is polluted and engrossed by this concupiscence; or, to express it more briefly, that man is of himself nothing else but concupiscence."

Similarly the *Westminster Confession* declared, in its sixth chapter, that by their sin Adam and Eve " fell from their original righteousness, and communion with God, and so became dead in sin, and wholly defiled in all the faculties and parts of soul and body. They being the root of all mankind, the guilt of this sin was imputed, and the same death in sin and corrupted nature conveyed to all their posterity, descending from them by ordinary generation. From this original corruption, whereby we are utterly indisposed, disabled, and made opposite to all good, and wholly inclined to all evil, do proceed all actual transgressions." It is very difficult to see what room is left for any subsequent operation of grace, when human nature is held to be so completely depraved: but there is no doubt about the consistency of this doctrine of utter depravity with the doctrine of double predestination. Grace is simply a name invented to cover a part of the play-activity which God, the Maker and Mover of puppets, has devised for Himself.

There is some relief from the oppression of this sorry scheme of things when we turn to the teaching of St. Augustine and of those who were more truly his followers. St. Augustine held that the condition of Adam before the Fall was not merely one of innocence, but that, by a particular endowment over and above what was essential to his human nature, he was placed in a state of original righteousness. "The first man had not that grace by which he should never will to be evil; but assuredly he had that in which if he willed to abide he would never be evil, and without which, moreover, he could not of free choice be good, but which, nevertheless, by free choice he could forsake. . . . And if that man had not forsaken that assistance of his free will, he would always have been good; but he forsook it, and he was forsaken."[1] When he sinned, Adam lost this super-endowment and very grievously corrupted his essential human nature. St. Augustine refrained, however, from pronouncing that the ruin was complete. Something was left for the divine grace to work upon, great though the degree of corruption was acknowledged to be. "Which of us can say that by the sin of the first man

[1] *On Rebuke and Grace*, c. 33.

free will perished from the human race? Through sin
liberty indeed perished, but it was that liberty which
was in Paradise, of having a full righteousness with
immortality; on account of which loss human nature
is without divine grace, since the Lord says, ' If the
Son shall make you free, then shall ye be free indeed '
—certainly free to live well and righteously. For free
will did not so far perish in the sinner but that by it
all men sin, especially they who sin with delight and
with love of sin; they will what pleases them." [1]

It is true that the measure of free will which St.
Augustine allows to fallen man amounts to very little,
and indeed that he seems to take away even that small
measure when he is proclaiming the irresistible nature
of grace: but the important point is that his desire to
establish the fact of man's retention of some degree
of will-power after he Fall delivers him from the
charge of teaching the total depravity of human
nature. He did not believe that that nature was completely dehumanised: but he held that there was, on
the contrary, just enough of its inherent constitution
remaining to serve the redeeming purpose of divine
grace. By the Fall man's will became attached to evil;
by grace it could be directed towards the good.

St. Thomas Aquinas and his school accepted the
main outlines of the Augustinian teaching on this
matter, distinguishing with greater clearness between
the natural and the supernatural elements in the para-
disal condition of Adam, and recognising that the loss

[1] *Against Two Letters of the Pelagians*, c. 5.

of the latter introduced grave disorder into the former; and the same position was taken later by the Jansenists. It is also the teaching of the Thirty-nine Articles of the Church of England, the ninth of which states that " original sin standeth not in the following of Adam (as the Pelagians do vainly talk), but it is the fault and corruption of the nature of every man that naturally is engendered of the offspring of Adam, whereby man is very far gone from original righteousness, and is of his own nature inclined to evil, so that the flesh lusteth always contrary to the spirit; and therefore in every person born into this world, it deserveth God's wrath and damnation." Here, while the degree of corruption resulting from the Fall is stated to be great, there is a deliberate avoidance of any assertion to the effect that it is complete, as the Westminster divines held it to be. Seeking to conform the terms of the Article to their own theological standards, they insisted upon revising the statement that " man is very far gone from original righteousness, and is of his own nature inclined to evil " so as to make it read: " Man is wholly deprived of original righteousness, and is of his own nature inclined only to evil."

The mildest of the three types of theory is that which was taught by the Greek and the early Latin Fathers on the basis of New Testament doctrine. Reasserted and systematised by the followers of Duns Scotus in opposition to the sterner doctrine of the Thomists, it was ultimately included in the findings of the Council of Trent. This theory recognises that Adam's sin was followed by the loss of a supernatural bias towards good, and it regards the nature of man as consequently enfeebled: but it knows nothing of man's total depravity, or even of his depravity. Having recorded in its fifth session that Adam forfeited holiness and righteousness by his transgression, and was changed for the worse; that this loss and deterioration was transmitted to his posterity; and that the remedy is in Christ alone; the Council of Trent proceeded to state, in its sixth session, that in Adam's offspring " free will, attenuated and bent down as it was in its powers, was by no means extinguished "; and it further interpreted its meaning by declaring in its Catechism that when man was formed from the earth, he was " so created and qualified in body as to be immortal and impassible, not however by the strength of nature, but by the divine gift. But as regards the soul of man, God created it to His image and likeness; gifted him with free will; and so tempered all his motions and appetites that they should at all times be subject to the control of reason. He then added the admirable gift of original righteousness. . . . When Adam had departed from the obedience due to God, and had violated that prohibition, ' Of every tree,' etc., he fell into the extreme calamity of losing the sanctity and righteousness in which he had been placed, and of becoming subject to all those other evils which are detailed more at large " (in the passages referred to above, viz. the wrath and indignation of God, physical death, and captivity to the devil).

This form of the doctrine of the Fall seems to be in the closest agreement both with the teaching of the New Testament, considered as a whole, and with the patent facts of life. In spite of theological assurances to the contrary, man knows he is not wholly bad; and in spite of the tempting consolation of scientific pronouncements he knows he is not what he ought to be and what he might be. As Barrie once aptly expressed it: " The life of every man is a diary in which he means to write one story and writes another, and his humblest hour is when he compares the volume as it is with what he vowed to make it." The tokens of his greatness are found in the fact that he desires to do well, and in the sorrow produced by his failure. His weakness is only too plainly recorded in the ground of his sorrow. His nature, that is the nature of the whole human family, is neither utterly depraved, so as to be incapable of restoration to the good which he desires; nor is it essentially good, so as to be in no need of restoring aid. Grievously handicapped though he is, by reason of the evil which has intruded itself into God's creation, by the original sin which is the resultant of the sins of all his forefathers, and most of all by the actual sins which were his own, man is yet redeemable, if only some great appeal and some sufficient help were available from outside him. On no merely theoretical ground, but on the basis of what has happened repeatedly since the Son of God became incarnate, we can affirm that such aid is available, and that, whenever men choose to lay hold upon it and use it aright, they are redeemed.

The doctrine of prevenient grace stands for the truth that in this work of redemption, as in all the righteous deeds of the life that follows after its achievement, God is always the first to move. No sinner can ever turn to God without first being claimed by prevenient grace—known also as operant, antecedent, and exciting grace, because the activity is that of God alone—and enabled to respond to the claim by means of subsequent grace—known also as co-operant, concomitant, and assisting grace, because divine and human activities are now conjoined. St. Chrysostom thought differently. He declared that " it is necessary for us first to choose goodness, and when we have chosen it, then God introduces goodness from Himself. It is our function to choose beforehand, and to will, but it is God's function to finish and to bring to completion." So too thought the Semi-Pelagians, who asserted that man himself is able to take the initiative, and that the grace of God is given as the reward of quest, whenever with all their hearts men truly seek Him. Accepting this opinion, and recognising that it involved the introduction of the conception of meritorious action, the Franciscan Schoolmen sought to meet the difficulty by drawing a distinction between ' condign ' merit, which is the result of a discharge of recognised duty and meets with payment according to a contractual agreement, and ' congruous ' merit, which merely puts an inferior into such a position that his superior is enabled appropriately to bestow upon him some mark of his favour. But, apart from any question of the validity of this distinction, it is a mistake to suppose either that God waits for man to turn to Him or that man is able so to turn; or again that God waits for the converted man to initiate righteous actions, or that he is able so to do. God is the source of all our life, both physical and spiritual; and, just as He alone maintains the beating of our hearts, so there is no thought or desire of good in us that does not owe its origin to Him.

The only conceivable ground for denying the doctrine of prevenient grace in connection with the redemption of sinners is to be found in the observation of the fact that, whereas some men are obviously sought out and claimed by God, very many more appear to be required to undertake the task of searching after God. Moreover, it is not infrequently the case that their quest proves so long and so difficult that they are moved to exclaim, " Verily thou art a God that hidest thyself. " This strongly suggests that, while prevenient grace is bestowed upon the few, the imparting of grace is much more commonly the sequel to human effort and appeal. On examination, however, it will be seen that God and man are active together in the second case no less than in the first, and that God Himself is at all times the originator of the joint activity.

Where chosen men are relentlessly pursued by the

Spirit of God, and are claimed in a memorable spiritual crisis which is inevitably regarded as a divine act of apprehension, there is not only no doubt about the prevenience of grace, but it appears to be the case that the man himself makes no contribution to the result. Psychological inquiry shows, on the contrary, that the seemingly sudden surrender to God in response to a compelling power follows a more or less prolonged period of unconscious or partly conscious incubation, during which a controversy is being carried on between the Spirit of God and the spirit of man; and, although it is customary to speak of the wearing down of the sinner's resistance, it is more truly a matter of winning a consenting mind by the operation of love, so that mental readjustment and intellectual apprehension may follow. The actual conversion is the crisis and conclusion of a divine-human struggle, initiated by God in order to set the man's soul in the right direction and to win it to the undertaking of its proper travail.

Where, on the other hand, men themselves are seen to make what appears to be a self-initiated and self-sustained search after a hidden God, and to arrive at a state of peaceful communion which admits of being regarded as the reward of their own successful endeavour, the difference of method ought not to blind us to the fact that it is equally the result of the will and the patient purpose of God, and that it is just as truly contrived and initiated by His love as in the cases where He is known to be the seeker. Instead of a dogged pursuit there is a persistent attraction: instead of a smiting correction of conscience in respect of particular faults there is an enlargement of desire for general righteousness; and to stern insistence upon the abandonment of error and sin there is added a winning invitation to service. But in all these cases, as in the others, it is God who is secretly working upon the spirit of man, and it is God who, in co-operation with the man upon whom He has laid His hand, advances him towards the vision and the fellowship which are the goal.

Prevenient grace is never irresistible, great though its constraining power is often seen to be; and, when once its operation has been initiated by God, it passes into the co-operative work—synergistic, not monergistic—of subsequent grace. St. Paul's declaration, " I was not disobedient unto the heavenly vision ", though it refers rather to the exercise of free will during his early post-conversion life, cannot be altogether dissociated from the initial act of self-surrender which was his immediate response to the vision of Christ. And in order to make these important facts about operant and co-operant grace clear beyond all doubt, our Lord Himself once told three parables in rapid sequence, when He was explaining to His critics the reason for His association with publicans and sinners. In the first story the sheep that was lost was recovered by the Good Shepherd and brought back willy-nilly. In the second story the lost coin had no option in being found and restored by the woman from whose hand it had fallen. But, lest we should wrongly suppose that the search made by the Son of God, and by the men and women who seek the lost in His Name, is the end of the matter, Christ immediately went on to tell of the lost son; and in that third story He carefully avoided giving to the father any active share in the son's restoration. On the contrary He made it plain that the son must come to himself and of his own free will return to his home, so that we might be certainly informed that man's co-operation with God when prevenient grace has done its work is essential to the fulfilment of the divine purpose.

In the post-conversion life it is precisely the same, though the same superficial distinction is to be observed between actions that appear to be God-initiated and others that seem to begin with man. Sometimes it appears to a man that good works are prepared for him by God; and he performs them with a strong sense of acting in response to the direct bidding of God and of being guided and supported by His power. At other times he seems to be required to plan for himself and to put forth his own energy. Yet he knows that every suggestion of good that comes to birth in his mind is from God, and that every fraction of the power which he is able to exert comes equally from the God who claimed him and to whom he surrendered. There is a mysterious inner communing between the Spirit of God and the spirit of man, and a still more mysterious association between them in action; so that it is quite impossible to say where God's part ends and man's part begins. But though it happens sometimes that God's share is predominant according to the mind of the man in whom He is working, and sometimes the man's own share is predominant, he knows that the ultimate truth of the matter is that he has nothing of his own, but that it is God who is working in him at all times when he is occupied in righteousness. He knows this with growing assurance because he is living the life of prayer. By means of his daily and hourly intercourse with God he becomes increasingly certain of divine guidance and enabling, and is aware, though he can prove the truth to no one, that his whole life is divinely ordered and empowered.

It is for him in varying measure a reproduction of the earthly life of prayer and activity which was lived by our Lord Himself when He walked among men. For the Gospels make it clear that Jesus Christ always waited upon the Father, committing to Him all His plans for His work, delaying action or moving forward according to the Father's appointment, and fully conscious at all times that the Spirit was working His works in Him. We read, for example, that He was ' driven ' by the Spirit, that He ' must needs ' do this or that, and that He would sometimes postpone a suggested action on the ground that His hour was not yet come. He marvelled, and was apparently deeply gratified, at the insight of the centurion who assured Him, with a soldierly frankness, that he believed in His ability to heal his servant, because he also was a man ' under authority '; and in commending his great faith He declared His own subjective experience of the operation of the grace of God in His Humanity. This has been well stated by Dr. H. Townsend, when he says that in the reciprocal activity of prayer "Christ surrendered Himself completely to His Father's will, and He was conscious of inspiration as He did so. The infinite objective resources, which Paul would describe as the unfathomable riches of divine Grace, became accessible to Jesus, and His own powers of volition transmuted them to effect the Father's purpose. . . . The prayers, persistence, and sacrifice of Jesus were His own achievements, and they were His working out of the immanent resources of His Father's Grace both for Himself and others." [1]

[1] *The Doctrine of Grace in the Synoptic Gospels*, p. 70 f.

CHAPTER V

Grace, Habitual and Actual

IT may be well at this stage to recapitulate the results of our investigations in the previous chapters. After a rapid survey of the formulation of the doctrine of grace, in which we took account of the classic debates on the subject and noted the successive phases of its development, we attempted to answer the question: " What is grace? " Here we found that it is essentially the divine favour which is bestowed upon man, and that it takes the form of a beneficent personal influence which is brought to bear upon the spirit of man by the Spirit of God. It is not rightly conceived as the Holy Spirit Himself; it is not a commodity which is conveyed into man's being for the healing and rehabilitation of his nature; but it is the power of the Personality of the Creator working upon the personality of each of His creatures by the means which we commonly describe as personal influence. The fact that the Incarnation of the Son of God is the supreme act in the operation of grace, by which the fullest measure of personal influence is rendered possible, requires us to speak of grace as " the grace of the Lord Jesus Christ ". Next we considered the claim, which amounts to a very grave charge against the justice of

God, that He is responsible for an arbitrary discrimination between men, some of whom He predestinates to be the recipients of His saving grace, while the others are abandoned to the destruction which is their appointed lot as sharers in a corrupted nature. The various arguments used in support of this most immoral doctrine were examined and rejected; and the conclusion was reached that God's mercy is upon all men and that salvation is available for all, while the scheme of salvation includes the method of election to special privilege and responsibility, by which some are chosen to serve God's purpose of good for all. We then examined the question of free will, on the theological and practical side, considering the problem of the Fall of man and the results produced by it upon human nature, and accepting the positions that the distinction between prevenient grace and subsequent grace correctly discriminates between the two successive stages in the divine operation, that the doctrine of prevenient grace safeguards the truth of the divine initiative at all times, and that the doctrine of subsequent grace faithfully recognises the mystery of the co-operation between God and man, whereby man is enabled to bring forth the fruit of good works.

Before turning to the consideration of yet another pair of terms used in the exposition of the doctrine of grace, we ought to warn ourselves against the danger of supposing that there are various kinds of grace. All grace is divine favour, and it is one: but its operation is manifold, and it is a matter of great convenience and usefulness that the diverse purposes and results of the bestowal of grace should be differentiated by the attachment of qualifying terms to the constant term ' grace '. Thus, if any reader should feel disposed to protest against the introduction of further technical terminology, his protest may be accepted in so far as it provides a necessary warning against any misapprehension of what was in the minds of those who coined descriptive names: but it must also be pointed out that the results of very searching investigations of the successive stages of the work of grace are embodied in these terms, and that they have great theological and practical value.

The important distinction to which we now turn our attention received its first clear expression at the hands of St. Thomas Aquinas. It is the distinction between what is termed ' habitual grace ', or the relatively permanent grace which effects the healing of the soul and places it in a state of salvation, and the transient and recurrent grace which leads the soul to undertake particular activities and is therefore generally known as ' actual grace '. The latter we have already considered under its two forms of prevenient and subsequent grace. The former is the new part of our subject; and it deserves to be stated first in the words of Aquinas himself.

He believed that " Man's nature may be looked at in two ways: first, in its integrity, as it was in our first parent; secondly, as it is corrupted in us after the sin of our first parent. Now in both states human nature needs the help of God as First Mover, to do or wish any good whatsoever, as stated above. But in the state of integrity, as regards the sufficiency of the operative power, man by his natural endowments could wish and do the good proportionate to his nature, such as the good of acquired virtue; but not surpassing good, as the good of infused virtue. But in the state of corrupt nature, man falls short of what he could do by his nature, so that he is unable to fulfil it by his own natural powers. Yet because human nature is not altogether corrupted by sin, so as to be shorn of every natural good, even in the state of corrupted nature it can, by virtue of its natural endowments, work some particular good, as to build dwellings, plant vineyards, and the like; yet it cannot do all the good natural to it, so as to fall short in nothing; just as a sick man can of himself make some movements, yet he cannot be perfectly moved with the movements of one in health, unless by the help of medicine he be cured. And thus in the state of perfect nature man needs a gratuitous strength superadded to natural strength for one reason, viz. in order to do and wish supernatural good; but in the state of corrupt nature for two reasons, viz. in order to be healed, and furthermore in order to carry out works of supernatural virtue, which are meritorious. Beyond this, in both states man needs the divine help, that he may be moved to act well."[1]

Here it will be noticed that actual grace is referred to

[1] *Summa*, II. Pt. I. Q. 109, Art. 2.

only in the final sentence. All that precedes that sentence is concerned with man's need of habitual grace. Returning to the same subject a little later Aquinas says that: " In order to live righteously a man needs a twofold help of God—first, a habitual gift, whereby corrupted human nature is healed, and after being healed is lifted up so as to work deeds meritorious of everlasting life which exceed the capacity of nature. Secondly, man needs the help of grace in order to be moved by God to act. Now with regard to the first kind of help, man does not need a further help of grace, that is to say a further infused habit. Yet he needs the help of grace in another way, that is in order to be moved by God to act righteously, and this for two reasons: first, for the general reason that no created thing can put forth any act, unless by virtue of the divine motion. Secondly, for this special reason— the condition of the state of human nature. For although healed by grace as to the mind, yet it remains corrupted and poisoned in the flesh, whereby it serves *the law of sin* (Rom. vii. 25). In the intellect, too, there remains the darkness of ignorance, whereby, as it is written (Rom. viii. 26): *We know not what we should pray for as we ought*; since on account of the various turns of circumstances and because we do not know ourselves perfectly we cannot fully know what is for our good, according to Wisdom iv. 14: *For the thoughts of mortal men are fearful and our counsels uncertain.* Hence we must be guided and guarded by God, who knows and can do all things. For which reason also it is becoming in those who have been born again as sons of God to say: *Lead us not into temptation,* and *Thy will be done in earth as it is in heaven,* and whatever else is contained in the Lord's Prayer pertaining to this. The gift of habitual grace is not therefore given to us that we may no longer need the divine help; for every creature needs to be preserved in the good received from Him. Hence if, after having received grace, man still needs the divine help, it cannot be concluded that grace is given to no purpose, or that it is imperfect, since man will need the divine help even in the state of glory, when grace shall be fully perfected. But here grace is to some extent imperfect, inasmuch as it does not completely heal man, as stated above."[1]

The conception of habitual grace, which is set forth in this passage, has become the very foundation of the Catholic expression of the doctrine of grace; while it is generally rejected by Protestant theologians as false. No way of complete reconciliation between the two camps has so far declared itself; though it is true to say that a more accurate knowledge of what is believed on the one side and the other is contributing to the elimination of exaggerated statements of the existing difference, and to a recognition of divergent stresses which to a slight extent account for the opposition.

Since the doctrine of habitual grace is closely connected with that of justification, the best approach to

[1] *Summa,* ii. Pt. I. Q. 109, Art. 9.

its consideration is the institution of a comparison of the opposed statements of the sequence of events which is believed to take place when a man is converted to Christ by the operation of grace, prevenient and subsequent. According to the scheme of thought which was formulated by the Protestant Reformers and is held by Protestants generally, there is produced in him, by the grace of God, the kind of faith that is termed 'fiduciary faith'. This is a faith of the heart rather than of the head, though it carries with it a certain intellectual content. It is a general conviction that God is prepared to overlook, or to cover up, man's sins, for the sake of Christ who died on his behalf; and it is a personal trust, issuing in an act of surrender, whereby the general conviction is given a specific application. It is the outcome of "the inner disclosure of God's gracious love to the heart of one and another man to whom He chooses to reveal himself."[1] It involves no theory of the Atonement, and no acceptance of any credal statement: but it reveals a conjunction of heart and mind in a simple but fervent expression of the faith that "I am saved, through the blood of Christ". As a result of this fiduciary faith, and through this alone, the justification of the sinner follows immediately. For Christ's sake he is accounted righteous by God; his sins are covered, so that he is discharged from their consequences. Yet he is not changed in his nature, but only in his moral disposition and in his liberty. The concupiscence that was in

[1] McGiffert: *Protestant Thought Before Kant*, p. 29.

him before his conversion remains active as before, and will continue to issue in the commission of sins. But these sins also will be covered by the divine mercy, on condition of repentance, because he is now justified in the sight of God.

The Catholic scheme of thought, developed through the Middle Ages and formulated with authority by the Council of Trent, follows very different lines. It declares that the grace of God produces in the sinner who is being converted a faith which is dogmatic instead of merely fiduciary; and that it creates also certain signs of a sincere change of heart, such as fear succeeded by hope, love, contrition, and good resolutions. By dogmatic faith is meant a belief in the fundamentals of the Christian creed, resulting from the acceptance of the communication of the Gospel by means of which conversion has been produced. It does not denote any considerable theological equipment: but at the same time it takes account of the fact that the quality of a man's devotion is very largely dependent upon his conception of the nature of the God to whom he addresses himself. The association of accompanying signs of a change of heart with this dogmatic faith is commonly regarded by Protestants as introducing the idea of a meritorious earning of justification by the performance of works: but it would appear rather to correspond in some measure with that fiduciary faith which is insisted upon on the Protestant side, though it is clearly wider in its scope. It certainly delivers the Catholic scheme from any charge of stressing unduly the intellectual element of the God-given qualifications for justification.

The justification that follows, when the grace of God has produced the required preparatory dispositions, is regarded by Catholic theology as working a twofold change. It cancels the sins of the converted man, and it imparts to him an interior sanctification by means of habitual grace. Whereas Protestant theology teaches that the sins are covered, and that, though the sinner is not really righteous, he is accounted righteous because the righteousness of Christ is imputed to him, Catholic theology insists that the sins are cancelled, and that the corrupted nature of man is healed. He is therefore not fictitiously regarded as a righteous man, but he actually becomes such by participation in the divine spirituality. This healing and participation are held to be immediate in cases where the preparatory dispositions include that perfect penitence for sin which is known as contrition. In all other cases they are necessarily conveyed by the sacrament of baptism, which is also administered even where contrition is present, since contrition is normally accompanied by a desire for baptism.

The subject of sacramental grace is to be considered in the next chapter, and may therefore be passed by at this point. Our concern now is not with the means by which this sanctifying or habitual grace is imparted, whether mediately by the method of baptismal regeneration or immediately by the direct action of the Holy Spirit, but with the nature of what is termed habitual grace, and with the question whether the result which it is held to produce in the soul is a reality or a theological fiction. The frequent use of the phrase ' infusion of grace' which is made by St. Thomas Aquinas inevitably puts us on our guard lest we should be betrayed into the acceptance of that quantitative idea of grace as a commodity which we have seen reason to reject; and the claim to participation in the divine spirituality seems to demand, and to admit of some measure of testing by observation of the lives of those who are said to have received habitual grace.

It must appear to any unprejudiced observer that the Catholic doctrine has the advantage of avoiding the suggestion of a certain artificiality which attaches to the Protestant statement. In its insistence upon the *covering* of sins, and the *imputation* of righteousness to one who has it not, the latter makes far larger demands upon the Christian thinker who knows that God is the God of truth. A measure of relief is afforded when it is explained, by some, that the sinner is justified not for what he now is but for what he will become by virtue of his association with Christ. The Redeemer is his guarantor, and it is understood that the righteousness which is imputed at the time of conversion will be progressively communicated through the rest of his life. But there is no guarantee of length of days for the fulfilment of the promise; nor indeed is there any certainty that the converted man who is permitted to live long will not fall away from the Faith, if we are to judge by the facts of life rather

than by the theological system which denies them.
The way of escape for the Protestant who would avoid
this difficulty would appear to lie in the frank recognition of the necessity for associating with justification
the idea of the intimacy of the union that begins at
once to exist between Christ and the sinner who has
been restored by Him, so that he is able to develop
the conception of the change that has come over him,
and of the newness of life that is conveyed to him.
This has been admirably done by Dr. A. S. Peake, in
words which afford hope for a large measure of reconciliation with the Catholic position, however strongly
its terminology may be objected to. He writes as
follows:[1]

" The apostle tells us that if any man has realised
this mystical union with Christ ' he is a new creature,
the old things have passed away, behold they have become new.' There is, first of all, the change in man's
status before God. The old condition was one of guilt
and condemnation, the new is one of forgiveness and
justification. In two striking verses Paul has asserted
this connection between the union with Christ and the
believer's status before God. Putting it in a negative
form, he says: ' There is no condemnation for them
that are in Christ Jesus.' Putting it in its positive form,
he speaks of being ' justified in Christ '. Now here we
confront a well-known difficulty. We are told that
God justifies the ungodly. The term which the apostle
uses means ' to declare righteous '; it is the opposite of

[1] *Christianity: Its Nature and its Truth*, pp 290–292.

' condemn ', as we see from the passage: ' It is God
that justifieth, who is he that shall condemn? ' Does
God, then, declare the ungodly to be righteous? Does
not this statement mean that God declares something
to be true which, as a matter of fact, is false? This
charge of immorality has often been urged against
Paul's teaching. I believe, however, that when we have
understood it, it really does not lie open to such a
criticism. We are not moving in a realm of fiction.
Paul's language is paradoxical, but it must be read in
the light of his fundamental conception. This is that
a man is justified in Christ—that if he is in Christ
there is no condemnation for him. But the very fact
that the union with Christ has taken place has carried
with it the ethical change. The man who is in Christ
is a new creature, and it is the new creature who has
become such through mystical union with his Saviour
who is declared to be righteous. He who was ungodly
has now ceased to be so. It is not while he is ungodly
before he has become one with Christ that he is so
described, but after the union has been effected and he
is ungodly no more. Hence we must not wring the
last drop of meaning, as some are disposed to do, out
of the expression ' justifies the ungodly ', but recognise that Paul is here using language which, from a
popular point of view, excellently expresses his meaning. We should none of us, I presume, object to say
that God declares the sinner righteous when he believes in Christ, but we should not wish to be taken
to mean that his faith had produced no radical change

in his condition. In other words, justification is a result
of the mystical union. It holds a secondary and not a
primary place in Paul's doctrine of salvation. But it
may be said, does not Paul refer justification to faith
as its cause? Certainly he does, but that in no way
contradicts the doctrine I have just been expounding.
For the union with Christ is itself the result of faith,
and since this includes justification, we may speak of
God's declaration of innocence as resting either upon
union with Christ, which is its immediate, or faith,
which is its more remote cause."

The use of the terms 'ethical change', 'mystical
union', and 'radical change', in the above passage is
of first importance, and raises the question: " Is it possible that these phrases mean the thing that is characterised by the Catholic as the infusion of habitual
grace? " It is very easy to take offence at the use of
the phrase 'infusion of grace'; but what exactly does
Aquinas mean by it? Are we sure that he thought
of an actual inpouring of some thing which would
produce a medicinal effect upon the soul? A Presby-
terian divine has noted the great difficulty of describing spiritual operations without resort to metaphor,
and has usefully drawn attention to the fact that, when
various metaphors are employed, they have a way of
blunting one another, so that none of them is to be
singled out and its particular meaning unduly pressed.
After examining a number of the metaphors employed
by him, he concludes that " Aquinas found the same
difficulty which others have found in defining grace,

and does his best to protect himself from being understood in any semi-materialistic sense."[1] It is true that
Protestant theology prefers to think in terms of moral
change, while Catholic theology more daringly asserts
a change in the soul: but it is difficult to see that, in
their ultimate meaning, they are very far apart. For
both include belief in the Incarnation, and in its sole
efficacy as the means whereby man is delivered from a
state of fallenness and corruption to a state of abiding
fellowship with his Maker. The grace of the Lord
Jesus Christ, laying hold of a man, transforms the
man himself; and, if there is a moral reformation
which declares itself to the friends of a converted man,
it is only because he is a new creature, now living in
grace, in a state of salvation. He enjoys a new status
in God's sight, and he lives the life of a changed man,
because something has happened to him, through
grace; so that, if the Catholic theologian asserts that
the man has received the gift of habitual grace, and
that because this has been infused, or added, or imparted, or bestowed, his soul is now close-knit to Christ
and participates in the divine spirituality it seems to be
an excellent way of stating a profound mystery which
we naturally desire to understand as far as human
thought and language can convey it to us. If the
language used suggests to some people a quasi-physical
soul, and a quasi-physical grace poured into it by the
healing Spirit of God, we must recognise, and perhaps
regret, the apparent inevitability of such misinterpre-

[1] Wotherspoon: *Religious Values in the Sacraments*, p. 129.

tation of the metaphorical language which we are bound to use: but it may well appear, on consideration, that the misinterpretation has in no way diminished the essential truth which the metaphor was intended to convey. And in its practical working and psychological value it is a very good thing for a man to think of his soul as having been restored so as to fit him for communion with his God, knowing at the same time that he is capable of forfeiting the habitual grace that has been given to him, and so of reducing his soul to its former state of degradation and thereby losing his fellowship with God.

The practical test of the truth of the Catholic statement must be found in the observation of the lives of those to whom habitual grace is said to have been imparted. If the soul is indeed restored to health and vigour and made capable of being stimulated by actual grace to the performance of deeds of righteousness, this will declare itself in the way which the Protestant scheme of things is eager to mark; and it most certainly does. Bad habits and evil practices are abandoned; good habits are formed, and charitable deeds are freely undertaken. But there is something which is even more important, because it is more inward and more fundamental. In place of attachment to worldly things, a new spirit of devotion and worship declares itself, revealing the fact that the soul which was formerly not functioning in a healthy manner is now vigorously alive. No more satisfactory method of explaining this appears to be available than that which is furnished by the doctrine of sanctifying, or habitual, grace.

Further important differences remain, however, between the Catholic scheme of thought on this subject and some of the systems which are widely, though by no means universally, held on the Protestant side. Whereas Protestantism, in some of its most characteristic forms, holds that certain knowledge of inclusion among the saved, complete uniformity of status, and the impossibility of defection and loss, attend all those who have been justified by faith, uncertainty, inequality, and defectibility, are affirmed on the Catholic side. On the one side is the static conception of a privileged condition which is unchanged and unchangeable, once it has been established. On the other side is the dynamic conception of a condition, privileged indeed but conditional, which is capable both of increase and growth, and of diminution and loss.

As to the possession of certain knowledge of salvation by each one who has been justified, there is a difference of emphasis rather than an absolute contradiction. It is agreed on both sides that there are people to whom a particular assurance has been vouchsafed: but, whereas the tendency on the Catholic side is to limit such cases to the number of those who have received an objective assurance, as, for example, the dying robber on the cross, the other side would greatly enlarge the number by insisting upon the equal validity of subjective assurance. While, however, it is not possible to rule out completely the authority of subjective

H

assurance, it is necessary that we should be reminded of the grave danger of self-delusion, and also that we should be warned against the arrogance that often treads very close upon the heels of assurance. And this has been done consistently and authoritatively on the Catholic side, and with equal insight and definiteness by many writers on the other side. Thus the Council of Trent affirmed that: " As no pious person ought to doubt respecting the mercy of God, the merit of Christ, and the virtue and efficacy of the sacraments, so each one, when he regards himself, and his own peculiar weakness and indisposition, may entertain fear and apprehension concerning his own grace; inasmuch as no one can know with a certainty of faith, which cannot be subject to mistake, that he has obtained the grace of God."[1] Similarly on the other side Ian Maclaren pointed out that: " The Spirit's witness *comes from God*, therefore it is veracious, divine, omnipotent; but the Spirit's witness from God *is in man*, therefore it may be wrongly read, it may be checked, it may for a time be kept down, and prevented from showing itself to be what it is."[2] And an admirable statement of the Catholic position, which seems to justify it beyond all question, by setting it firmly upon a scriptural basis, is found in *The King's Book; or, A Necessary Doctrine and Erudition for any Christian Man,* which was issued in 1543. In its treatment of *The Article of Justification*

[1] Session VI. c. IX.
[2] Sermons Preached in Manchester, Series I, p. 66.

this book asserts that: "All phantastical imagination, curious reasoning, and vain trust of predestination, is to be laid apart. And according to the plain manner of speaking and teaching of scripture, in innumerable places, we ought evermore to be in dread of our own frailty and natural pronity to fall to sin, and not to assure ourselves that we be elected, any otherwise than by feeling of spiritual motions in our heart, and by token of good and virtuous living, in following the grace of God, and persevering in the same to the end. And this St. Peter exhorteth us to make our vocation and election sure and stable. And Christ saith, He that persevereth unto the end shall be saved. And in Revelation of St. John, Be faithful unto death, and I shall give thee the crown of life. Wherefore when we be once elected and admitted unto God's service (as is aforesaid), and have received our justification in baptism, or be restored thereunto by true penance, then must we continually walk after Christ, bearing our cross, and increasing in His grace by good works; and so doing, proceed, go forward, and increase in our justification, according to the saying of St. John, He that is just, let him be more justified. For as the grace of God, and the gifts thereof, that is to say, faith, repentance, dread, hope, charity, with other fruits of the Holy Ghost do increase in us, so do we wax and increase in our justification."

It follows from the dynamic conception of habitual grace that there may be as many degrees of ' justification ', according to the last sentence of the passage just quoted, or, as it would be better to say, of 'sanctification', as the number of created souls. Catholic theology visualises the sons of men, here and in the life beyond, as moving forward on a long line of spiritual progress, each occupying his own more or less advanced position according to the correlative factors of the divine beneficence and the receptivity and energy of the particular soul. Protestant theology, on the other hand, pictures something in the nature of a spiritual socialism, by virtue of which all souls which are justified are accounted not only equally dear to God, but equally endowed, equally blessed, equally active, and equally developed. Reaction against the medieval exaltation of the Blessed Virgin, and of the saints in general, is partly responsible, no doubt, for this insistence upon equality in the sight of God. But for all that it is a position which is hardly tenable by any Christian who has learned the elements of the humility which belongs to his calling. The final equality of all the saints, when they have arrived at their ultimate perfection, is a matter which may be left to the speculative powers of those who choose to expound it: but for the present, and for a very long time to come, it will undoubtedly seem to most Christians who consider the matter with any care and with any proper feeling, that there is a great gap between themselves and some of the good men and women they have known, to say nothing of the Blessed Virgin and the Holy Apostles.

Finally, it is an article of the Calvinist creed that

none of those who are justified is able to fall from
grace. Since justification follows on predestination,
according to this creed, it is clear that no other sequel to
justification could be accounted possible. Nor is it legi-
timate to suppose that what is meant is that salvation
is assured however evil the life of a justified person
may be, though some have allowed themselves to be
forced into making such an assertion. The good life
is held to be as certain, in the case of one who is
really justified, as the end for which he has been predestined. The answer in the case of any who are
seen to fall from grace is obviously a declaration to
the effect that they were not truly predestinated.

In those parts of the Protestant world where the
doctrine of predestination is not held, and among
Catholics generally, there is a greater measure of freedom to face the facts; and the power to lapse from a
state of grace is frankly acknowledged. It is important to recognise that the doctrine of habitual grace
makes full provision for the exercise of this freedom.
The grace which rehabilitates the soul as a part of the
process of justification is differentiated from actual
grace as being relatively permanent, whereas the latter
is transient. But the retention of habitual grace is conditional upon the avoidance of grievous sin. By the
performance of righteous deeds it may be increased;
by the commission of mortal sin it may be lost; by
the remedy of absolution it may be restored. All this
seems to accord most accurately and most reasonably
with the results of the observation of the course of

life of those who are 'in Christ'. There is a steady growth in sanctity in a minority of cases; in the great majority of cases there is a succession of alternating movements, backwards and forwards, with every indication of a strenuous conflict; and in the other cases there is a cessation of effort and a consequent falling away from grace.

CHAPTER VI

The Means of Grace

THE personal influence of God, which is grace, is brought to bear upon men either by the direct action of the Holy Spirit working within them, or by means of mediating agencies, which are known in consequence as the means of grace. In the general experience of mankind these means are found in the physical and animal world, in human personalities, and in the creative works of such personalities. God speaks through the power and the beauty of the material universe and through the countless stages of the life which reaches up to man; He speaks through man himself yet more clearly and strongly; and He continues to speak through the books, the music, and the art, which men produce.

It was through the sights and sounds of the mysterious world of Nature that man first apprehended the God who made it. The strange and the uncanny things which he encountered were for a long time the chief indication to him of the presence of the Supernatural, together with the demonstrations of Power which were provided by thunderstorms, rivers in flood, earthquakes, and all the mighty threatenings of natural forces. Gradually, however, the significance of the quiet beauty and the glorious majesty of Nature began to declare to men's minds other and truer thoughts of God; and, while they were still affected to an unusual degree by extraordinary phenomena, the lesson of the starlit sky and of the unfailing return of the time of the almond-blossom did not escape them. The unwonted obstinacy of an animal conveyed to Balaam the warning grace of God; and some peculiar glory of the heavens uplifted the heart and understanding of the prophet Ezekiel; but men were already learning to consider the lily of the valley and the beauty of the dove's breast, and to let the grace of God steal into their hearts through their apprehending observation of such things. It is still God's way to speak to men through the beauty of His handiwork, and to convey His grace to them for healing and comforting, for strength and for purity, for the quickening of conscience and the stimulation of thought, by means of sunsets, and the reflection of trees and hills in deep water, and fields rich with flowers, and snow lying white upon the mountain-tops, and tender devotion in the eyes of a friendly dog. Such things are the elementary and universal means of grace.

Human personality has a double advantage over these, however, as a means of grace, in that it is both the fittest instrument of expression which God has made for the conveyance of His personal power, and the instrument which is most readily felt and understood by human beings. On God's side there is the fact that man was made in His image; on man's side there is the fact of identity of nature. Grace which is bestowed upon man results, as we have observed, in the transformation of human nature; and this transformation declares itself, not merely by the performance of good works, but by an increase of personal influence which is nothing else than the radiance of the grace which God has given. For the grace that is received cannot be concealed and reserved for private use. It must issue again through the personal influence of the man who has received it, even as it flowed forth from God when it was first bestowed upon him. And since religion is caught rather than taught, as we are often reminded, it will be recognised that to the quiet and often unconscious influence of men and women who are living in a state of grace a large part of the spread of religion is due. By the gracious influence of parents at home, of teachers and friends at school, and of the good people in various stations of life whom we meet in after days, we are always being fashioned by the hands of God Himself, through the agency of those who are His friends, and His means of grace.

In many cases these personalities which are enriched by the grace of God increase, and enlarge the range of, their personal influence, by adding the activity of doing to the state of being. By word of mouth they instruct and exhort their contemporaries; and they sometimes confer upon them and upon the generations that follow after them some enduring expression of the truth which they have learned or of the beauty which they have seen. In written words or in a picture, in a piece of sculpture, or in a building, or in some form of music, they are enabled by grace to record for the enjoyment and assistance of others something of what they themselves have been privileged to perceive; and so long as these things endure, they constitute means of grace to those who come within their power.

Such general agencies as these have been used by God from the beginning, and their use has marked every stage of man's long journey towards the truth. But "the grace of the Lord Jesus Christ", which represents so great an enlargement and intensification of the divine activity in the souls of men, while it continues to make use of these general agencies, has been so particularly associated with certain specially appointed means, that to a Christian the latter are instantly called to mind when the phrase "the means of grace" is heard. In the General Thanksgiving which is used in the Anglican Church we bless God for "our creation, preservation, and all the blessings of this life; but above all, for thine inestimable love in the redemption of the world by our Lord Jesus Christ; for the means of grace; and for the hope of glory". Here the means of grace are set in their proper place in relation both to the Incarnation of the Son of God and to the end for which that act was undertaken. They follow that supreme act of love which made them possible; and they are the ground of the hope of glory, to which they lead. Hence the phrase, whenever it is used, inevitably suggests to the Christian the preaching of the Gospel of Christ, the reading of the Word of God, the practice of prayer and meditation, the corporate worship of God, and the operation of the Church's sacramental system.

The communication of the Gospel, by means of the spoken word and the printed page, is obviously to some extent a particular use of the medium of human personality and of the work of human personality to which reference has just been made. But it is also very much more than that. The man and the book make up the human element, which is dwarfed by the spiritual value of the message which they are employed to convey. The treasure is carried in earthen vessels, and the quality and variety of the vessels is plainly to be seen when the treasure is displayed: but the power and the gift of grace is found in the treasure itself in this case, rather than in the human bearer of it. ' Saving truth ' is the phrase which best expresses the nature of the treasure; and ' inspiration ' is the term which best explains the ability of the human agent to convey the truth, and the ability of those who hear and read to recognise its divine source and to receive it. The gifts and the fervour of an inspired preacher and teacher of the Word certainly play their part in that commendation of the truth which is the conveyance of grace into the souls of the hearers; and the ability of those who are inspired to write down their record and commendation of the truth in noble and moving language plays its part again in the work of securing that emotional and intellectual approval by virtue of which grace is able to effect an entrance. But the power of the truth itself far exceeds the power of the gifts of those who commend it, and is the means by which the love of God ' finds ' man and wins him. ' Hearing sermons ' may become an unprofitable exercise to the hardened sermon-taster; and the diligent reading of the Word of God and of devotional literature based upon it may be undertaken in such a spirit as to miss the grace which rightly belongs to it. But the preaching and reading of the Word are none the less to be regarded as one of the chief agencies employed by God for the redemption and edification of the souls of men, and they are to be used in conjunction with each other, as combining to effect the one result. " The ancients had a feeling ", writes Dr. Inge,[1] " which was not entirely prejudice, that the most intimate and spiritual teaching should be oral, and not from books. No doubt it is the same feeling which makes so many persons prefer listening to speeches or sermons, rather than reading books. They need the sense of immediate contact with the personality of the speaker. Now in reading the Bible, or any other great book of devotion, we are not deprived of this immediate contact. The same Holy Spirit, who inspired the pages which we are reading, is ready to help us to understand and profit by them."

[1] *The Bible and How to Read It*, p. 45f.

The practice of prayer and meditation is to be regarded as at once a result of grace already received and a means to its increase. The soul which lacks grace is not willing to undertake the work of prayer, except when it is driven to do so by bodily dangers and worldly needs. Lacking grace, it normally lacks the desire and power of prayer, and is therefore precluded from receiving grace by that particular means. The soul which has been made to share in the divine spirituality by the addition of habitual grace is thereby rendered capable of prayer and is given a spirit of eagerness to exercise its capacity. In so doing it grows in grace. " He that hath, to him shall be given: and he that hath not, from him shall be taken away even that which he hath." (St. Mark, iv, 25.) Moreover, since the soul is educated by its converse with God, and comes gradually to a truer knowledge of itself and of its needs, and to a greater desire for its own perfection, its increasing capacity makes it possible for God to bestow His grace with a proportionate increase. The result is seen in the advancing sanctity of all who give themselves to prayer, and in the special graces that are added to those who excel. Some suggestion even of a development of power in the petitionary and intercessory use of prayer is found in the biblical statement that " the supplication of a righteous man availeth much in its working " (St. James, v. 16); and this reminds us that the impetratory aspect of prayer ought not to be lost sight of by those who judge it to be wise to emphasise the truth that prayer is communion with God. But the mystery which attaches to it is even greater than that which belongs to the growing sanctification of those who pray; and it is with prayer as a means of grace to the latter end that we are here concerned.

The most impressive of all the results of diligence in the performance of regular acts of prayer is the extension of the spirit of prayer over the whole life, so that the specific acts are caught up and bound together in a chain of unceasing prayer. According to Christian standards and the power of the grace of God this result is intended to declare itself in the life of every soul which Christ has claimed. As Canon A. L. Lilley has put it: " For the less spiritually developed religions prayer is a natural act, or rather a series of discontinuous acts, of the natural man. For Christianity it is a continuous spiritual state within which separate acts, indeed, find their place, and to the support and even the gradual formation of which they can contribute. But the simplest act of prayer of the Christian type is already an effect of divine inspiration, and it is not their mere repetition, however frequent, but their separate and varied representation of a continuously inspired state of soul that constitutes them authentic instances of prayer." [1]

In addition to the private maintenance of the activity of prayer, every Christian is required to merge his prayer-life in the corporate worship of the Church. By so doing he discharges his obligation to contribute

[1] *Prayer in Christian Theology*, p. 8f.

to the strength and quality of that worship, he receives from it again a definite stimulus to his private work of prayer, and grace is added to him for the sanctification of his soul and for its excitement to good works. It is not enough for him to pray in solitude, for the Church to which he belongs is under obligation to discharge, on behalf of God's Creation, that unceasing worship of the Creator which is at once His due and man's highest glory. Together with the Holy Angels and the spirits of just men made perfect, the Church on earth is privileged to join in the adoration of the Triune God, which ceases not day and night, consecrating stone and wood and metal to the advancement of its purpose, employing art and music and ceremonial action for its assistance and adornment, and yet so as ever to worship in spirit and truth Him who is Eternal Spirit. Together with the daily prayers of all its members, uttered in the secrecy of their own hearts, the Church offers the Daily Office as a corporate oblation, incumbent upon the sacred ministry and all religious orders and communities; and for the continual and thankful remembrance of the Sacrifice which once for all achieved man's redemption it makes its eucharistic pleading and offering at its altars, presenting its members, soul and body, before the throne of God, under the merciful covering of the Saviour whose life is there bestowed upon them anew. In their own tongues, and with much liberty in the ordering of local rites and ceremonies, the various parts of the Church yet combine to make a great corporate act of worship day by day, where all is conformed to the spirit and general order of the worship of the early Church, and all continues to be offered in and through the Lord Jesus. It is in this that the nature and function of the Church is most truly declared; and it is through this that grace is multiplied upon all the members of the worshipping Church, the more abundantly where the worship is direct, and innocent of subjective self-consideration.

Finally we come to the Church's sacramental system, which plays so large a part in the divine conveyance of grace that in the minds of many Christians ' the means of grace ' is practically equivalent to ' the sacraments of the Church '. While this equation limits unjustifiably the range of the means of grace it bears witness to a true apprehension of the Church's distinctive character. For the organisation which is the Church is differentiated from all other human organisations by the fact that it is of divine institution and that it is endowed with supernatural life. Other human organisations frequently reveal some measure of correspondence with divine law: but in none of them is there found the historical immediacy of institution which belongs to the Church, in none of them is there the same degree of prescription of form and of way of life, in none of them is there an equal permanence and stability, and in none of them is there anything approaching the degree in which the Church draws its life from the spiritual realm.

The Church on earth is a society of people whose

citizenship is in heaven; and its double habitation is unified by means of that sacramentalism which is the chief characteristic of its way of life. This results from the Incarnation of Him who created it and is for ever the Head of the Body. When the Word became Flesh, it was finally declared that the physical universe is not only not alien to God, but that it is capable of being used by God in conjunction with the Spirit in such a manner as to promote God's spiritual purposes. When, after His crucifixion, the incarnate Son of God burst the bonds of death and rose again from the tomb in a Body of glory, it was revealed that the physical universe, which groans and travails in pain together until now, is destined to be transformed by redemption and resurrection so as to become the perfect instrument of the Spirit. In the Church's stewardlike dispensation of God's loving-kindness and grace, it makes large use, therefore, of divinely appointed material things and associated action and prayer. Water, and bread and wine, and oil, in particular, are used by it so as to become the effectual signs of the spiritual gifts which God bestows upon His people through the Church's agency. And from these central and essential sacraments it is learned that the Christian life is lived wholly in a sacramental setting, which both declares the loving presence of the Living God, and serves to convey His manifold blessings.

By moral and spiritual co-operation with these sacramental means of grace the members of the Church

I

are progressively sanctified. The forgiveness of sins and the imparting of sanctity and power are available for all ' the saints ', who are potentially, by virtue of their inclusion within the Body, what they actually become by the operation of the Holy Ghost. But this is no automatic result, produced by the working of a heavenly elixir committed to the power of the priesthood. It demands the disciplined surrender and sustained co-operation of the Faithful, though it is achieved not by human merit but solely by the grace of God. As a good steward of the manifold gifts of God the Church is required to exercise authority over its members and to take every precaution against the abuse of its free gifts. It is governed in its action by certain general and far-reaching principles, which it is free to apply, directly and without self-contradiction, in the enactment of local disciplinary regulations; and, having exercised the fullest measure of care which is possible to human judgment and control, it must leave the ultimate responsibility for spiritual fitness and desire to the souls of its individual members, never ceasing to teach, to warn, and to encourage.

Essential as the sacramental system is to the life of the Church, and full of value as it is to the spiritual and moral life of the members of the Church, it yet admits of grievous misunderstanding both by those who administer and use it, and by those who criticise it from without. The prescription of formulae and the use of material substances and customary cere-

monial actions cannot fail to suggest in some quarters
a strong kinship with magical practices; and the charge
that sacraments and magic are identical is frequently
brought against the Church, not without a show of
justification from the teaching of some of those who
have erroneously explained the nature of the sacraments they have sought to recommend. Dr. C. C. J.
Webb has drawn attention to the fact that at the stage
at which the moralisation of the conception of a supernatural excellence of some kind added to the original
nature of a man has taken place, " not only does the
tradition still persist that things other than men, things
which are not subjects capable of moral predicates at
all, may yet receive such a supernatural excellence in
addition to their original nature; but even with respect
to men the *grace* bestowed upon them has sometimes
been described in a way which raises serious difficulties
from the point of view of the moral consciousness.
Thus it has been regarded as something which has
predestinated the elect person to salvation, antecedently
to the doing by him of either good or evil; or as something communicated to him through certain material
substances endowed with a sacramental virtue as
means of grace. We must be careful here to speak
exactly and not to misrepresent the views to which we
refer. Certainly neither was predestinating grace
thought to fail in at least ultimately sanctifying its
object, nor sacramental grace to be effective of salvation where the right moral dispositions could be present
and were not, or where actual sin had supervened;

unless, indeed, this in its turn should have been re-
moved by repentance and forgiveness. Yet there has
been a constant and urgent need of an effort on the
part of theologians who accepted the traditional language to answer the objections that predestinating
grace is arbitrary, and sacramental grace magical,
or, in other words, that the recognition of either
is offensive to the enlightened moral consciousness." [1]

The difficulty lies on both sides of the sacramental
action—on the side of the Church which administers
the sacrament and thereby communicates the grace
which is associated with it, and on the side of the
recipient of the sacrament and its grace. So far as the
administrative action is concerned there is the appearance of constraint of the divine power by the
observance of a technical procedure, or, to put it quite
popularly, the performing of a spiritual transaction by
virtue of the possession of "ability to work the
trick". And so far as the reception of the gift is
concerned there is the appearance of a considerable
degree of independence of the moral and spiritual
capacity of the person concerned. It will be necessary
to give some consideration to these two matters in
turn.

The most obvious difference between the Church's
sacramental action through the priest, and the activity
of the magician in the lower ranges of religious prac-

---

[1] *Problems in the Relations of God and Man*, p. 91f.

tice, are these. The magician acts for himself and by means of the knowledge and power which he claims to possess as an individual; whereas the priest acts in the name of the society which has duly commissioned him as its representative in the matter. The magician represents himself to be in possession of certain powers of control over forces which belong to a chancy world impinging upon man's life but beyond the reach of normal human direction; whereas the priest is known to be a man under authority, whose actions are pre-scribed by the society which he represents, in con-formity with directions which are believed to have been received by that society from the Supernatural Order itself. If, therefore, the charge of magic is brought by the critics of the Church's sacramental system, it is the Church that must be challenged as the magician, and not the individual priest. That in-volves the critics in the necessity of examining the 'magician's' credentials. They must make full in-quiry into the Church's claim to be doing what God has ordained for the good of His people rather than to be acting in the spirit of one who knows how to make God do things in spite of Himself. Is it, for example, God's will that people should be cleansed from sin and fed with spiritual food and drink? Or is it to be supposed that the Church has conceived the desirability of God's performance of these things and has come to believe that it knows how to compel Him to do it?

A further doubt is expressed by those who advertise

their inability to understand why the Church is so confident about the efficacy of its action. Granted, they say, that God is ready to do these things, and that He does normally perform them in answer to the prayers of the Church, what security is there that the thing that is said to be done is indeed always done, when the right words and actions are used? Is there not an overweening confidence and an unwarranted rigidity about the whole matter, in view of the fact that human nature so frequently fails to rise to the height of a great occasion? What justification is there for the assertion that the sacraments infallibly effect the purpose which is in the mind of the Church, at all times and in all places, *ex opere operato* (i.e. through the act performed)? If this criticism means that the state of soul of the recipient of the sacrament can never be certainly known, the answer is, of course, that the Church is fully aware of the fact, and also that it expressly teaches that impediments to the receiving of sacramental grace will deprive the soul in which they exist of the benefit which it would otherwise receive, and, where there is a wilfully sacrilegious approach to a sacrament, will result in its injury. But if the reference is to the possibility of a lack of spirituality in the minister of the sacrament, or of his moral unworthiness, then the Church replies that God may nevertheless be trusted to confer upon the recipient of the sacrament the grace which he seeks, as a result of its administration by the Church. The sacrament, that is to say, is not the priest's private concern but the concern of the Church in whose name he ministers. The members of the Church clearly cannot be cheated of that which they seek from God through the Church because of secret faults or spiritual sluggishness in the priest who ministers to them. If the priest be duly authorised, and if he duly performs his office, then it must be held that God's covenant with the Faithful is fulfilled, through the performance of the sacramental act.

The second part of the difficulty lies, not in the possible unworthiness of the recipient of a sacrament, but in his immaturity, as, for example, in the case of a very simple and dull-witted communicant, or, more clearly still, in the case of an infant brought to baptism. It appears to critics of the sacramental system that, unless there is some obvious measure of moral and intellectual congruity on the part of those who share in the Church's sacraments, the whole system is reduced to the level of the medicine-man's art. But the criticism is invalidated by the most elementary knowledge of the psychology of influence. The grace that is conveyed by means of sacraments is no different from the grace that is conveyed by any other means. It is the work of the Holy Spirit on the spirit of each recipient; and it is, therefore, very far from being dependent upon intellectual gifts and a ready perception of spiritual values. In the case of the humblest communicant it will be conceded that there is some conscious perception of what is happening. The manner of ordering the celebration and administration of the sacrament makes it impossible to suppose that its meaning is wholly lost upon any. But there is abundant justification for the claim that human personality is able to apprehend beyond the powers of conscious mind and reason, and that the influence and work of the Holy Spirit penetrate to deeper levels of man's being.

This is the very ground of the institution of sacramental usage. It is the particular application of that general use of the physical universe which God makes when He bestows grace through the sacrament of Nature. On God's side it is a profound intensification of that use, made possible by the Incarnation; and on man's side it is a means of bringing to the aid of the intellect, whether developed or undeveloped, the fullest use of the senses and of the subconscious mind. As to the case of infant baptism, it is to be regarded as the initiation of a spiritual process in an embryo personality which is already receptive of the mother's influence, and cannot, therefore, be held to be inaccessible to the influence of the Holy Spirit; and the use of the sacramental matter, which is water, while it makes no appeal to the senses of the child, is justified not only by the necessity for preserving identity of administration in the case of adults and infants alike, but by the fact that its appeal is to the responsible adults through whom the Holy Spirit largely works in the early life of the child. It is the practice of the Western Church to complete, by Confirmation, the process which was initiated in Infant Baptism, at an age when the Holy Spirit's direct action on the life of the child may be held to have developed so far as to exceed the measure of His mediated action through the influence of those who entered into the sacramental bond on behalf of the child at its baptism.

CHAPTER VII

The Achievements of Grace

Among the many illustrations provided by our Lord in order to convey to simple understandings some apprehension of the character of the Kingdom of God, the most striking in connection with our subject is the Parable of the Mustard Seed. This seems to be intended to direct attention to the similarity between natural growth and spiritual growth, and at the same time to suggest, by the abnormality of the growth which is described, a distinction between the known and expected limits of natural growth and the altogether unknown and unexpected limits of spiritual growth. In method they are alike; for in both cases it is God who gives the increase, which is by the silent and steady accession of life, claiming and fashioning the material which it draws from its earthly environment. In results they are unlike; for, whereas seed sown in the earth invariably produces a plant which conforms more or less closely to a standard type, the souls of men are liable to record in themselves a growth which is altogether disproportionate and unlooked for. Natural law certainly operates in the spiritual world, but it is inadequate as a criterion by which to form reliable expectations of the dimensions which growth may there achieve; for, under the Christian dispensation, the amazing growth of the mustard seed in the parable will be paralleled by such remarkable developments of character that men will be constrained to regard them as the result of the introduction into the life of man of something higher than nature, which raises the natural man to more than natural heights.

There are many who challenge the distinction between nature and supernature, in the interests of a philosophical monism, and through an unwillingness to allow the identification of the supernatural with the miraculous and the consequent enlargement of the use of the latter term. They prefer to regard what is called the supernatural as continuous with the natural. The one is held to reach up into the other; and it is accounted unnecessary, and indeed impossible, to draw a dividing line between the two. But without contradiction of a philosophy which thus seeks to reduce to an ultimate unity the practical dualism of the moral and spiritual life, the theological doctrine of grace demands the recognition of a distinction between the natural and the supernatural, for its own purpose, on the basis of revealed truth and observed fact; and it insists upon a differentiation between natural goodness and supernatural goodness as essential to any true estimation of man's moral activities. There is no goodness in man that is not of God: but in some men there is found a goodness of such distinctive excellence that it becomes necessary to recognise its origin by applying to it a distinctive name. The former is the goodness which is still possible, through grace, to the human nature which God created, though it has been weakened and corrupted by sin and has not yet laid hold of the redemption which is in Christ Jesus; the latter is the goodness which exceeds the powers of human nature, until that nature has been endowed with the grace of the Lord Jesus Christ.

The virtuous character had been much discussed in both East and West before the birth of the Christian religion, and many true things had been said about it. Of the various analyses of the virtuous life which existed at that time early Christian thinkers seized upon the code in which Cicero had popularised the teaching of Plato and Aristotle. This grouped together Temperance, Fortitude, Justice, and Prudence, as the four essential virtues which characterise the moral man. He must be self-disciplined so as to control his bodily passions; he must know how to show courage in the face of danger; he must be equitable in his dealings with his fellow-men; and he must be understanding in practical affairs so as to be able to order his life with the wisdom of a prudent man.

Though vision inevitably outstripped performance, there were many who strove to practise these virtues in the pagan world which surrounded the early Church, as there are still some who endeavour to practise them in the pagan world which lives in the midst of the Church of to-day. Grace was not denied them then, and it is not denied them now; and the results are not to be forgotten when the achievements

of grace are being reckoned. But both the interpretation of these natural, or moral, or cardinal virtues, as
they were called, and their translation into action were
enormously advanced when Christianity took them
over into its scheme and supplied them with a supernatural basis. This basis consists in what are known
as the theological virtues of Faith, Hope, and Charity.
In the course of his lengthy exposition of the virtues
St. Thomas Aquinas provides an admirably terse summary of the separate characters of these three virtues,
in which the achievements of grace make their most
unmistakable claim to recognition. He teaches that:
" A virtue is said to be theological from having God
for the object to which it adheres. Now one may
adhere to a thing in two ways: first, for its own sake;
secondly, because something else is attained thereby.
Accordingly charity makes us adhere to God for His
own sake, uniting our minds to God by the emotion
of love. On the other hand, hope and faith make man
adhere to God as to a principle wherefrom certain
things accrue to us. Now we derive from God both
knowledge of truth and the attainment of perfect
goodness. Accordingly faith makes us adhere to God
as the source whence we derive the knowledge of truth,
since we believe that what God tells us is true: while
hope makes us adhere to God as the source whence
we derive perfect goodness, that is, in so far as, by
hope, we trust to the divine assistance for obtaining
happiness."[1]

[1] *Summa,* ii. Pt. II. Q. 17, Art. 6.

It is a serious error to suppose that these three theological virtues were simply added to the four cardinal virtues, so that, while pagans had only four virtues, Christians were able to count themselves in possession of seven. The introduction of virtues which have God for the object to which they adhere inevitably transformed those other virtues to which they were added. Moreover, the theological virtues are the internal spring from which the others, in their changed nature, must proceed. They are in no sense just set down by the side of the others in order to supplement them and so to make up the complete list. The difference between natural goodness and supernatural goodness is not the difference between the conduct of those who are capable of displaying only the cardinal virtues and that of those who are able to display the theological virtues also: but it is the difference between those who practise the cardinal virtues as they were received in the pagan world, and those who practise both the theological virtues and the cardinal virtues as they are interpreted by Christians.

Thus, in adopting the scheme of the cardinal virtues from the pagan world, the Church transformed them, at the hands of St. Ambrose and St. Thomas Aquinas in turn, by giving them a new direction. Whereas they had formerly constituted a summary guide to practical conduct for men who would behave themselves rationally in this present world, with a clear appreciation of the difference between the condition of a man and that of an animal, they were related by the Church to the spiritual order of things revealed and effected by Jesus Christ; and they were interpreted so as to serve the needs of men who were travelling to a far country and had their eyes set on the goal. Temperance became the surrender of all that is worldly, and the true direction of the affections; Fortitude was enlarged so as to include the endurance and courage of the soul in the presence of opposition and spiritual dangers; Justice was attached to the thought of the service of Him who is the Father of all, and to the idea of complete abandonment of self-interest; and Prudence had an eye, not to worldly security and the avoidance of economic and social pitfalls, but to the guardianship of the pilgrim soul. Thus the phenomenon of the character of the Christian saint was interpreted to the Church and to the World; and the interpretation served as a useful guide to those who, while they belonged to the fellowship of the saints, had not yet succeeded in reaching that extraordinary degree of sanctity, or supernatural goodness, for which the name of 'saint' was soon reserved.

Not only were the cardinal virtues thus transformed, and filled out with a new content, however, but a new power was available for their practice. Grace enlarged the sense of obligation, and, at the same time, it strengthened the whole personality, so that the gap between vision and performance was reduced and even bridged, though the vision had carried them so far onward. Saints, and saints in the making—all alike revealed in their lives, according to their degree, the

achievements of grace. Many of them had been retrieved from lives of shame and great wickedness by
seemingly miraculous conversions; many of them had
been changed from moral weaklings to characters full
of courage; many of them had laid aside cruelty and
arrogance and had become notable patterns of love and
humility; and all of them exhibited a spirit of detachment and other-worldliness, an impressive sense of
power in their spiritual assurance and their moral
mastery, a charity which was entirely new to the
world, and a spirit of fervent joy which was unaffected
by the condition of their lives. A familiar passage
from Justin's *Apology* summed it all up in memorable
words which admitted of no contradiction by the
critics to whom they were addressed. " We that once
took our pleasure in impurity, now embrace chastity
alone. We that used the arts of magic, now do conse-
crate ourselves to the good and unbegotten God. We
that, above all, loved the ways of wealth and plenty,
now bring all we own into the common stock, distributing alike to all in need. We that were full of
mutual hatred and thoughts of murder, ready to
refuse to all save kinsmen the rights of hospitality,
now, since the appearing of Christ, share hearth and
home; we pray for our enemies, and seek to persuade
those that wrongfully hate us, to the intent that they,
living agreeably to the fair precepts of Christ, may be
of good hope to receive from God, the Lord of All,
that which we also hope to obtain."[1]

[1] *Apology,* I. 14.

Since those early days the number of Christians who deserve to be known as saints cannot be said to have shown an increase proportionate to the extent of the extent of the spread of Christianity. As the Church has grown in size it has raised the moral standards of the heathen world at the cost of a serious declension in the general level of its own sanctity; and the appearance of a true saint in its midst has tended to become something of a rarity. Yet the achievements of grace which were registered in the saints of the early Church have never ceased. Saints have appeared in successive generations of the Church's history, and will doubtless continue to appear to-day and to-morrow, as outstanding evidence of the fact that the grace of God continues to be operative and to work with undiminished power. What is transacted in a phenomenal degree in their lives is being continued, in varying degrees according to the capacity and the co-operation of the human instrument, in the lives of all those who are called to be saints. Where this is forgotten, and the grace of supernatural goodness is not looked for and claimed, there is little to distinguish the life of the Christian from the life of the non-Christian in moral and spritual power; for grace never works irresistibly and automatically. But where the achievements of grace in the formation of the saintly character are remembered, and it is remembered also that grace is available for the production of a similar result in the lives of all who enjoy the communion of the saints, much happens, and will always

K

happen. The saints are the abiding guarantee of this truth.

In addition to the creation of the Christian character, which is its greatest achievement, the grace of the Lord Jesus Christ imparts to chosen men and women particular *charismata*, or spiritual gifts, for the edification of the other members of the Body. These are gifts of power for the purpose of pastoral administration and rule, for the purpose of teaching and exhortation, and for the ministry of consolation and healing. The work of the priest and the schoolmaster and the doctor, now shared by three different professions, is nevertheless a unity, by virtue of the constitution of that human nature with which all three of them have to deal; and this unity was for a very long time proclaimed by the Church, which discharged the threefold task by means of the *charismata* committed to some of its members. The differentiation between those who now exercise the different parts of this ministry has resulted inevitably from the great increase of knowledge that has come to each of the three departments, and from the consequent necessity for specialisation: but it would not have been attended by the very obvious disadvantages from which it now suffers, if it had been brought about as a more marked differentiation of function within the Church and not as, to a large extent, a double defection from the Church.

While these special gifts are not necessarily associated with a high degree of personal sanctity, it is usually found that the saints are each possessed of one

or more of them in addition to the supernatural goodness which constitutes their claim to sainthood. The
calendar of the saints includes many royal persons,
bishops, abbots and abbesses, priests, and others, who
have borne wise and kindly rule over the people committed to their charge; many great scholars, teachers,
and preachers, who have interpreted the Faith and advanced the knowledge of it among the Faithful; and
many who have practised the arts of nursing and healing, and of general ministration to the poor and
distressed. And outside the Church's roll of the saints
there are unnumbered names of Christian men and
women in whom the achievements of grace have been
made known by their possession of gifts in these
various ways and by their most devoted use of them.

Thus the whole world has benefited by the gifts
which grace has bestowed upon the members of the
Church; and it would not be unnatural to advance a
comprehensive list of the benefits thus received by the
nations in substantiation of the claim that grace has
many and great achievements to its credit. The re-
straint of tyrannical rule and the institution of the
Christian monarchy, the deliverance of minds op-
pressed with error and unworthy fear, the relief of
distress in all its various forms, and the promotion of
godlike compassion on man and beast—these and the
many other works which belong to the Christian insistence upon the recognition of the value of human personality, are achievements of the grace which has
wrought unceasingly in the followers of the Lord of

Grace. But, great as they are, these are to be regarded merely as the by-products of the work of grace. They have happened by the way, in the course of the pursuit of its ultimate goal and its greatest achievement, which is the production of the Christian character, the creation of yet more saints. The saints themselves will abide; their works which they have performed through grace will abide also, in the characters of the saints who follow after them.

INDEX

149